Date Due			
J4'42			
Jan 5			
May 13 '43			
May 26 '43			
May 30 '45			
Apr 23 4 6			
May 7 4 6			
May 27 4 6			
May 28 4 6			
May 28 4 6			
May 28 4 6			
May 28 4 6			
May 28 4 6			
Jan 27 '75			
Jan 14 '75			
℗			

↓

WHY

EUROPE

FIGHTS

↑

also by

WALTER MILLIS

ROAD TO WAR

THE MARTIAL SPIRIT

WHY

EUROPE

FIGHTS

by WALTER MILLIS

WILLIAM MORROW
AND COMPANY
NEW YORK 1940

WHY EUROPE FIGHTS

PRINTED IN THE UNITED STATES OF AMERICA
BY QUINN & BODEN COMPANY, INC., RAHWAY, N. J.

FOREWORD

THE PURPOSE OF THIS BOOK IS A VERY modest one. It offers no contribution to history. Utilizing the material readily available on any good reference shelf, it attempts nothing more than a simple, but factually accurate, interpretation of the broad complex of forces and events which led, within twenty-one years from the end of the last great war in Europe, to the outbreak of another. The history of those years is yet to be written. But if in the meanwhile this brief account is of some value as a review of their salient features and as an aid in clarifying ideas of why Europe is again at war, it will have done all that the author asks of it.

It endeavors to be objective. It does not attempt, however, to conceal the author's conviction that certain tendencies and national policies were more definitely retrograde, more immediately responsible for the new war, than others. All studies of this kind must be written from some point of view. It is the author's view that the rise of totalitarian absolutism, particularly in its German form, was the major disaster of the period and the most direct assignable "cause" of the conflict, but that this "cause" can only be considered against the backgrounds of economic dislocation, bitterness and defeat out of which the totalitarianisms arose. These backgrounds, also, the book endeavors to present, leaving to the reader all final questions of moral justification.

W. M.

April 19, 1940

INTRODUCTION to the Second Printing

SINCE THIS BOOK WAS FINISHED, THE totalitarian war machine, revealing a more terrible power for destruction than anyone had imagined, has overrun Norway, Holland, Belgium and France, reducing the whole West of Europe to physical or moral ruin and leaving Great Britain (as this second edition goes to press) standing as a kind of last, beleaguered outpost of a democratic system which now finds its main base in North America. The war has been brought to the United States with an urgency which no one could have foreseen even a few months ago, and our people have been thrown into a fury of belated preparation and divided and uncertain counsels before a danger more immediate and far more formidable than any of us had realized.

This account of why Europe is at war has suddenly become a sketch of some of the reasons why, sooner or later, the United States may be at war—for no one can now shut his eyes to the possibility. In describing the backgrounds of Europe's crisis, it now describes the backgrounds of what has already become a crisis for the United States; and in so doing perhaps it will be a help in resolving our divisions and clearing away our uncertainties. It records, at any rate, some of the steps by which I have sought to do this for myself, and draws the general picture out of which my own conclusions have grown.

They have led me to an attitude toward this conflict unlike that which I have taken toward America's participation in the war of 1914-18. Five years ago, in my *Road to War*, I severely criticized that episode —whether rightly or wrongly I leave it to others to say. But I do not believe that that analysis, whether it was right or wrong, can be or ought to be applied to the present crisis. For all its superficial similarities, I believe that this issue differs both in degree and in kind from that with which this nation was confronted in 1914. It has grown out of a very different history—developed in a different way and presented us with an infinitely more immediate, fundamental and searching problem.

This book seeks only to give a general view of the backgrounds; it offers no advice as to how that problem should be met. But I cannot repress the hope that it may, in however small a measure, contribute something toward securing that the people of the United States, whatever they may do, will do it with courage and consistency. The one thing about which I care intensely is that the United States, facing what is unquestionably the most critical moment in its own history and in the history of the civilization of which it is a part, should face it with clear realism, unflinching confidence in its own convictions and complete unity.

W. M.

June 19, 1940

PART ONE
THE NEW WORLD

1. WAR'S END

THERE IS NO REAL BEGINNING FOR anything in history, just as there is never any end. But wars always have to begin somewhere; and the best place at which to begin the story of the new war in Europe is with the signing, on June 28, 1919, of the great treaty of peace which was supposed to have ended the last one. It was a brilliant summer day in Paris; and in the near-by town of Versailles the sun glittered on the lance-heads and bayonets of the great masses of victorious troops which lined the broad avenue leading up to the vast and splendid palace of Louis XIV. From about midday the cars had been rolling along it, carrying the generals and statesmen, the politicians and diplomats and experts and lesser officials of all the Allied powers, come to take part in or to watch the solemn ceremony that was to mark the formal ending of the World War. They entered the palace gates through more masses of soldiery; they passed up the grand stairway, lined with a guard of honor ready to salute the greatest ones, and slowly they filled the famous Hall of Mirrors where the

3

signing of the Treaty of Versailles was to take place.

It was just five years to the day since the shot had been fired at Serajevo, with which the Great War began. Among the gathering crowd were many of the leaders who had guided the Allied peoples and their armies through all the horror and suffering that had followed. They remembered the dark days of the war, its frightful losses and terrible weariness. They remembered the 900,000 dead soldiers of England, the 1,300,000 dead Frenchmen, the 600,000 Italians and the many thousands more from other Allied countries sacrificed in that tremendous struggle. They remembered the millions of wounded, and the countless others who had suffered in all the ways that war can bring. They remembered the desolate countryside of Northern France over which the German armies had trampled in their invasion, the ruined factories, the sunken ships and all the other colossal costs of war. And they remembered the tremendous moment when the great victory, which had so often seemed impossible, had come at last. They were triumphant and they were bitter; they were resolved that someone should pay for all that horror and that it should not happen again. Through the past five months they had been at work, amid all the hurry and confusion and disagreement of the Paris Peace Conference, deciding what they would do with the victory and what sort of world they could rebuild out of the ruins of the war. That work was finished; and the Treaty of Versailles, in a big, leather-bound official copy, now lay upon a small table in the middle of the hall in which the peace delegates and the spectators were assembling.

The men who wrote the Treaty of Versailles and the other treaties that went with it were trying to do two rather different things. They were trying to end the war, punish Germany and make her helpless to fight again. At the same time they were also trying— and most of them were probably trying sincerely—to put together in some better way all the fragments of countries and peoples and governments which the vast upheaval of the war had left behind, to make a new international system in which the nations could live more comfortably with each other and free from the fear of another such enormous disaster. Both these efforts were written into the treaties. But the whole of this final ceremony had been planned to mark, not the rebuilding of the new world, but the great military triumph of the Allies over a beaten and helpless Germany.

The Germans had been allowed to have no word in the making of the treaty. When it was first shown to their representatives, Clemenceau, the fierce old man who had led France to victory, had told them bluntly: "It is neither the time nor the place for superfluous words. . . . You have asked for peace. We are ready to give you peace." And today the Allied leaders were ready to insist that the Germans take what had been given them. The Hall of Mirrors was the room in which Bismarck, in 1871, had chosen to proclaim the new German Empire he had created and so to emphasize the defeat and humiliation of France, which his armies were then overrunning. It had been chosen now in order to mark France's bitter revenge for that day, and to emphasize the deeper humiliation and more complete defeat which she and her allies had imposed upon the Germans. It was filling, by this time, with the official spectators; the delegates themselves were coming up the grand stairway, to the salutes of the guard of honor, thrusting through the crowd and taking their places at the great U-shaped table prepared for them in the central section of the hall. Clemenceau, with his hard, round head, his white walrus mustaches and black gloves, was in the seat of honor. He looked "small and yellow." Lloyd George, the clever and vigorous Prime Minister of Great Britain, and President Wilson, with his long and serious face, were nearly the last to enter; their seats were on either side of the French Premier. A group of French, British and American soldiers, to represent the armies who had fought and died to win the peace which these men were making, was prominently placed. The chatter quieted. "Bring in the Germans!" said Clemenceau with a snap.

Through a small side entrance the two German delegates were brought in, as if they had been criminals; they were seated at the lower end of the table, between the Japanese and the Brazilians and opposite the delegates of Peru, Ecuador and Liberia. Clemenceau called the meeting to order. "The signatures," he said, "will be given now, and they amount to a solemn undertaking faithfully and loyally to execute the conditions embodied in this Treaty of Peace. I now invite the delegates of the German Reich to sign." Nervously, and both deathly pale, the two men jumped up to do so. But they had to wait while Clemenceau's speech was translated. Then one of them found that his fountain pen wouldn't work and had to borrow another. Instead of being impressive, it was pitiable, and not even dignified. Many in the room only felt sorry for the Germans. They sat down again, and the Allied delegates, beginning with President Wilson, then signed in turn, with a marble bust of Athena, the goddess of wisdom, looking down upon them. Within thirty-five minutes it was finished; and just as Clemenceau declared the proceedings at an end, the guns began to thunder through Versailles and boom from the forts round Paris, and the world knew the Great War was formally over.

The two Germans were hurried away first through the same side door by which they had entered; but the others went out upon the splendid terrace where the famous fountains of Versailles had been set playing in the sun. Hundreds more were there, and when the chiefs of the three great Allied powers appeared the crowds burst through the guards to surround them in struggling and cheering masses. "Vive Clemenceau!" "Vive Wilson!" "Vive Lloyd George!"

Airplanes roared across the sky; the guns still thundered; while in Paris at the same time vast throngs
were in the streets for an all-day festival. Peace had
been made. The victory had been signed and sealed.
And when presently Clemenceau, Wilson and Lloyd
George climbed into a car and were borne off together, they were still the three most powerful men
on earth.

President Wilson that same day issued a message
to the American people:

> It is a severe treaty in the duties and penalties
> it imposes upon Germany, but it is severe only
> because great wrongs done by Germany are to
> be righted and repaired. And it is much more
> than a treaty of peace with Germany. It liberates
> great peoples who have never before been able
> to find the way to liberty. It ends once and for
> all the old and intolerable order under which
> small groups of selfish men could use the peo-
> ples of great empires to serve their ambition for
> power and dominion. . . . It makes interna-
> tional law a reality. . . . It lays the basis for
> conventions which shall free the commercial
> intercourse of the world from unjust and vexa-
> tious restrictions. . . . There is ground here
> for deep satisfaction, universal reassurance and
> confident hope.

But in Germany they did not think so; and one of
the few Berlin newspapers which had anything to
say at all began its article with the words: "Lest We

Forget!" The German people, it said, "will again strive to attain that place among the nations of the world to which it is entitled. Then, vengeance for 1919!"

So peace was made, and the new world order was proclaimed. It was a bitter and humiliating peace; but war—whoever starts it—is bound to be a bitter and cruel thing, and in a time filled with so much recent suffering, hatred, fear and triumph a more generous settlement would probably have been impossible. And this settlement (as it was embodied in the Treaty of Versailles and the treaties later signed with the other defeated powers) did at least try to establish a new working system under which the peoples of Europe could live and conduct their affairs with some justice and safety and contentment, and without again having to undergo such a horrible and shattering experience.

The system rested, of course, upon the complete defeat of the two great empires of Germany and Austria-Hungary, which had governed the whole of Central Europe, and upon the break-up of one of them. It assumed that these two empires had been solely responsible for starting the war, and it compelled them to sign, in the treaties, an admission of their "war guilt." Consequently, it began by almost completely disarming Germany (as well as Austria and Hungary) and by forbidding her ever to possess those weapons, such as airplanes, tanks, heavy artillery and submarines, without which it is impossible to

fight a modern war. It forbade Germany ever to
fortify her western boundary, so that she would
always be open to a quick invasion from France if
she should again threaten to start a war. And it presented Germany with an enormous bill for war damages. Nobody believed that Germany could actually
pay all the costs of the war. Nobody knew in 1919
how much she might in time be able to pay. But the
makers of the treaty believed that Germany ought
to pay as much as she could. The bill for damages,
or "reparations," was therefore made very large; but
the actual amount that would be collected was left
to be determined later, when the terrific wreckage of
the war had been cleared up, when ordinary industries had been got going again, and when it would
be possible to see what Germany's real capacity to
pay might be.

But all the rest of Central Europe had been torn
up by the war. The Austro-Hungarian Empire,
within which many different peoples speaking different languages had been held together, after a fashion
and with a good deal of hostility, in one working
combination, had already gone to pieces when the
Paris Conference first met. Czechoslovakia had already declared her independence. The Prince Regent
of Serbia had accepted the invitation to take over the
regency of the former Austrian provinces which
combined with the Serbs to form the new state of
Yugoslavia. Rumania had marched into the great
provinces of Hungary to which she believed herself

entitled. Italy had occupied the Southern Tyrol; while the small remaining portions of the former Austria and Hungary, from which these great slices had been lopped off, had already separated from each other under independent governments. Another country, Poland, which had been divided up and had disappeared from the map in the eighteenth century, had already revived, had declared its independence, and was seizing or claiming parts not only of Austria but of Germany and of what had been Russia. Still other parts of Russia were breaking off to declare themselves the independent states of Finland, Esthonia, Latvia and Lithuania.

These things had all happened by the time the Peace Conference met in Paris. It did not deliberately take Central Europe apart; but as the only strong center of authority in Europe it was immediately faced with the problem of arranging the fragments as best it could. Here it adopted the principle of "self-determination." Most people, even among those who believed that Germany had deliberately started the war, knew that no one nation could start so great a war unless things were seriously wrong to begin with; and it was widely believed that one of the deeper causes of the war had been the struggle of all these Central and Eastern European peoples to free themselves from the often harsh domination of the autocratic empires under which they had lived. It therefore seemed that one of the best ways of preventing the outbreak of a new great war would be to confirm all these peoples in their new liberty as independent and self-governing states. To the victorious statesmen at Paris it seemed so even more, because this would further weaken the two great powers they had just overcome.

So they went to work on the principle of "self-determination" to draw the boundaries of these new countries which had come into being. The trouble was that the various racial groups were everywhere so mixed together that sharp lines could not be drawn between them. The territory occupied by any one group often fell short of the strategic frontiers—rivers or mountain chains—which it must have if it were to be able to defend itself. And the economic resources and commercial organization by which all these peoples lived everywhere cut across the racial lines along which they had divided. The result was, for example, that "self-determination" for the Rumanians who were living in what had been Hungary meant that hundreds of thousands of Hungarians who were living in the same area had to pass under foreign rule. In order to give the new state of Czecho-slovakia both the military frontiers and economic resources it needed for survival, 3,500,000 German-Austrians who lived in the mountain fringes of the Czech territory had to be placed under Czech governance.

The intention was to give the principle of "self-determination" a general application, only modifying it here and there to take care of strategic and eco-

nomic necessities. But the modifications raised any
number of difficult issues, and it was not strange that
the Peace Conference, when it had to decide them,
usually decided them against Germany, Austria and
Hungary. In this way Germany, already disarmed
and under obligation to pay an enormous bill for
damages, also lost a good deal of territory and with
it many of her most valuable industrial resources.
The mines and industries of Silesia went to Poland.
The Lorraine iron mines went to France with the
restoration of Alsace-Lorraine; in addition, the coal
and iron mines of the Saar Valley were placed under
French ownership as reparation for the mines in
Northern France which had been destroyed by the
German armies. Austria became a small and mainly
agricultural state that somehow had to support the
great city of Vienna, which, as the capital of a huge
empire, had grown to a population of nearly 2,000,-
000. Hungary became another small agricultural
state, ringed by hostile nations enclosing millions of
her own people, and trying to maintain on slender
resources an expensive and backward landed aris-
tocracy; while everywhere the borders of the new
nations cut across long-established trade lines or raised
bitter "minority" problems.

But it was hoped that the new system would take
care of all the difficulties which this redrawing of the
map of Europe must clearly leave behind it. For at
the head of all, the treaties set up the League of Nations to safeguard and administer the new structure.

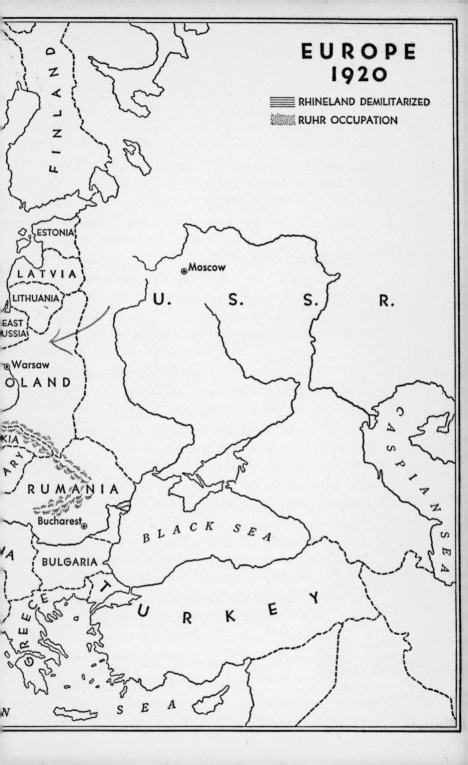

EUROPE
1920

RHINELAND DEMILITARIZED
RUHR OCCUPATION

FINLAND

ESTONIA

LATVIA

LITHUANIA

EAST
PRUSSIA

Warsaw

POLAND

U. S. S. R.

Moscow

CASPIAN SEA

KIA

ARY

RUMANIA

Bucharest

BLACK SEA

VA

BULGARIA

GREECE

TURKEY

N

SEA

The League would guarantee every nation against attack by its neighbors, and so make questions of armaments and strategic frontiers of less importance. It would protect the minorities which the treaties scattered through the new states, and so make their lot less hard, and less likely to cause trouble, than the lot of the formerly subject peoples who had been set free. It would decide as justly as possible the complicated border disputes between the new nations. It would make it possible for the victor powers to follow Germany in laying aside their own huge armaments, and would encourage them to do so. By providing an international control for the great water and rail communication lines through Europe, by working for the general equalization of labor conditions and living standards, by encouraging the reduction of tariffs, it would overcome the economic dislocations caused by the creation of so many new countries, and make possible a reasonably prosperous life for all. And it would be better able to do all these things, because the United States—a country more or less detached from the European struggle and so capable of looking impartially upon its problems— would be the League's strongest member.

This is what the new order announced by the booming guns at Versailles was intended to be. A Germany which had confessed herself guilty of starting the Great War would be totally disarmed and made to pay as much as possible of the costs. With Germany thus rendered harmless, the major foundation would be laid for peace elsewhere. The various principal peoples of Central Europe would be set free to live their own lives under their own governance with more contentment than they had known when subject to the former Austrian and Russian and German empires. Presently the machinery of economic life would be set going again; Germany would then pay off what she fairly could and in time return as an equal to the common association of all nations. Meanwhile France, made safe by Germany's disarmament, protected by the League of Nations and by a special treaty in which the United States and Great Britain would promise to come to her aid if she should be attacked, could reduce her own armaments. Under the shelter of the League a general disarmament would presently come. With the fear of military war eliminated there would be less reason for economic wars; tariff barriers could be thrown down and the nations could work together for a greater prosperity for all. And above everything, the strong authority of the League would stand to iron out, on the basis of justice and reasonableness, all the special difficulties and disputes that were bound to arise.

This is what the new world system was intended to be; unhappily, what the new world was intended to be and what it really was were two very different things. It was not true, to begin with, that Germany had been solely guilty of starting the war. The Germans did not believe it, and bitterly resented being

compelled to sign the "war guilt" clause; more than
that, few thoughtful men even in the Allied countries really believed it, either. Because Germany had
not been solely responsible, rendering Germany
harmless did far less than might have been supposed
to end the causes of war, which were present in all
the other great powers as well in some degree or another.

So far from being able to pay heavy damages for
the war, Germany at the moment could pay nothing
whatever. Her people were actually starving to
death in thousands as a result of the Allies' blockade
and all the dislocations of the war. The country was
in a turmoil of unrest, revolution, uncertainty and
misery; and the task of finding out what she could
fairly pay and setting her to paying it, so far from
proving quick or simple, was to drag on for years.

The new nations were not living their own lives
in freedom and contentment. All over the continent
of Europe the machinery of economic life was in a
state of almost complete breakdown. There were
minor wars, violences, revolutions on every hand.
There was a Bolshevist dictatorship in Hungary, and
a great fear everywhere that Bolshevism would sweep
out of Russia right across Central Europe in a vast
revolutionary wave. The countries were seizing territory from each other where they could and redrawing their own boundaries. And there was no strong
international authority in the League of Nations to
enforce order, to settle these disputes and assure

reason and justice and economic opportunity for all.

The tremendous power which the Allied statesmen had wielded at the Paris Conference seemed to be dwindling every day in mutual disagreements and confusions. The League was not finally organized until November, 1920, and then it was far from the institution which had been intended. Soviet Russia had been excluded. It meant that one of the great nations of Europe, whose policies and actions were bound sooner or later to affect everything that happened on the Continent, had no place in what was supposed to be the common council. The United States had refused to become a member; and the more or less impartial influence, which might have helped to guide the other powers to a reasonably fair decision of all the problems around them, was wanting. Even the special treaty under which Great Britain and the United States would have promised to come to France's aid if she were attacked was never ratified. Without this protection, the French had no desire to disarm, nor did any of the other victor powers. There was fear, bitterness, poverty and uncertainty everywhere.

Many of those who had watched the grand ceremony in the Hall of Mirrors had felt or foreseen all this. There was more sympathy for the Germans than there was enthusiasm for the victory. One witness thought that the general feeling was rather one of relief that the weary business was over than one

of satisfaction in the results. "Success," another told
a friend, "is beastly, isn't it?" and went away, "sick
of life." Like many others he realized that the first
task of the new world order would be to make a new
world order.

2. STRANGE TIME, STRANGE FIGURES

THIS TASK WAS TO TAKE ABOUT FIVE
years—the five years of confusion, of violence, of
great hopes and much despair that stretched between
the making of the peace and the making of the Treaty
of Locarno in 1925. The task was enormous. The
armies had to be brought home, demobilized and put
back to work; while the numerous little wars left
over from the great one—in several parts of Russia,
in Turkey, in Poland, in Ireland and elsewhere—had
to be fought out or brought to a stop. Russia, swept
by a great revolution which had destroyed nearly
everything of wealth, of power and of organization
in the country, had to find herself; while the other
nations had to decide what they would do about this

huge section of Europe, which had simply disappeared from the international community, but from which the revolutionary threat reached out to sap at the foundations of their own societies. The boundaries of the new states had to be settled; their governments had to be created and launched upon their work; their economic life had to be set going. The League of Nations had to be established. But until it should show the strength necessary to control European affairs, the various new and old nations felt obliged to group themselves together in some arrangement of alliances that would, if possible, keep the peace and afford some general measure of security and stability to the Continent. Finally, the problem of fixing Germany's reparation debt and compelling her to begin payment of it had to be settled; and it was to prove one of the most difficult and damaging of all.

The matter of Russia was solved very simply, though not, perhaps, very intelligently. The several small wars against the Bolshevists, fought by "White" Russian generals with money, supplies and support from the Allied governments, soon petered out against the savage resistance of Leon Trotsky's Red Army; and the Allies withdrew, leaving the wrecked and chaotic mass of Soviet Russia to herself. Because of their fear of Communist revolution and because they still hoped one day to collect the vast debts contracted in Czarist times, the Western powers refused to recognize Lenin's government. No ambassadors

were exchanged with Moscow; few foreign correspondents, even, were sent there by the great Western newspapers; and with the destruction of Russian
economic life, trade with the outer world almost
disappeared for a time. Russia was simply walled off
from the rest of Europe behind a curtain of fear,
ignorance and hostility.

In 1922 the other nations received a sudden and
unpleasant hint that this policy might one day prove
unwise. An international conference was called that
year at Genoa, to which the defeated as well as the
victorious powers were invited, in the hope of putting
all European affairs on a better basis. The Russians
were not particularly helpful; but while the main
negotiations were dragging along they slipped away
with the German delegates to the near-by resort town
of Rapallo and secretly concluded a separate treaty
under which the two nations settled the issues between them and agreed to resume diplomatic relations. The Western powers were shocked and angry.
They were horrified by the thought of what might
happen if the defeated Germans and the despised Bolshevists should join in a military alliance against those
who had won the war. It was plain that if Soviet
Russia ever did return to take an active part in European affairs, she might wield a tremendous influence.
But instead of trying to understand and work with
the Bolshevists, the Western powers preferred to go
on leaving them alone; the Genoa conference came

to nothing and it was years before Europe was to begin to learn the true importance of Russia.

It was less simple to deal with the unrest and violence which the Communist revolution in Russia had spread through the rest of Europe, or to prop up the new governments into whose weak and inexperienced hands the future had been entrusted. The treaty-makers had looked forward to the rise of free and democratic government everywhere out of the ruins of the two great Central European empires. Germany had declared herself a republic; so had Austria and Hungary and Czechoslovakia and Poland, and where monarchy remained in the older states it was liberal and constitutional monarchy. But the peoples in all these lands were not accustomed to democracy. In most of them the strongest and best-organized popular groups were the industrial workers. They had learned self-government in their trade unions; it was their representatives, in most of the new democracies, who took over the control of the governments at the beginning and tried to start them on a path of progressive social reform. Although they generally called themselves Social Democrats, their socialism was of a very mild sort, and they were no believers in revolution. But in most of these countries they were only one group out of many.

There were many other parties—farmers' parties, church parties, conservative parties supported by big landowners or industrialists, middle-class parties— usually in bitter conflict with each other. Around the

new governments there stormed every kind of violence and hostility. Everywhere there were active
Communist groups, calling for revolution, urging the
workers to strike and sometimes rising in bloody rebellion. There were hordes of demobilized soldiers,
out of work, disillusioned, and feeling restless and
empty now that the terrible excitement of the war
had passed. Formed, often, into armed bands, they
roamed the streets battling Communists, or threatened to settle by violence the border disputes left over
from the treaties. People were starving, weary, and
in the defeated countries embittered by the loss of
the war and the hard terms imposed upon them. The
reforms in the way of greater freedom, cheaper food,
higher wages and better living conditions which the
new liberal governments were trying to put into
effect were simply seized upon as the excuse for more
exorbitant demands by the violent radicals and were,
therefore, only more savagely opposed by the violent
reactionaries. Against all this the new democratic
governments had to struggle; and they had to struggle with no strong popular support behind them,
amid peoples with little real belief in democracy itself and, above all, with no money in their treasuries.

The Hungarian Republic collapsed altogether and
almost at once. Through most of 1919 a Bolshevist
dictatorship ruled in Hungary, expropriating the rich
and slaughtering its opponents by the hundred; and
when it was finally overthrown its successors slaughtered the Communists with almost equal savagery. In

the end Hungary became a monarchy without a monarch—for the Allies would not permit the former emperor of Austria-Hungary to reign again. Under Admiral Horthy as Regent its government returned to the firm control of the great conservative land-owning families. In Germany there was a Communist rebellion in 1919; and Munich, the capital of the big southern state of Bavaria, was for some weeks under a workers' soviet, until the army marched in and crushed the movement with much bloodshed. Then in the following year there was a rebellion of soldiers and monarchists in Berlin, and that was defeated only when the Berlin workers declared a general strike in defense of the republic.

It was a strange time, and there were many strange figures in it. One summer evening in 1919, just after the Bavarian Soviet had been destroyed, a queer little group of five men was sitting around a table under a gas lamp in a Munich beer hall. Four of them (with two others who were not there) had been founding a new political party, and they were asking the fifth man to join. There were countless little parties and movements and conspiracies being formed in Germany in those days; there must have been many other conferences like this one. These were obscure, restless young men with an amateur interest in politics. They hated their poverty and insignificance, they hated the peace treaties, they hated Socialists and Jews whom they thought of as having caused Germany's defeat, but they themselves had vague, half-socialistic ideas about the overthrow of financiers and capitalists and the creation of a great national community—something splendid and powerful that all Germans could admire and feel proud of and that would make everybody prosperous.

They had been holding obscure little meetings from time to time in Munich beer halls, spouting these ideas to audiences of a dozen or two; and their "party" now had the equivalent of about $1.50 in its treasury. The fifth man was the strangest of the lot. He was an infantry corporal—a lonely, unhappy, emotional man of thirty who had known nothing but poverty and frustration, who had dreamed of himself as having great talents as an artist, as a soldier and leader, and was bitter against a world that had failed to recognize them. An Austrian by birth, he had fought through the war in the German Army; he had been wounded and later gassed, and had broken down and wept when the news came of Germany's defeat. He had stayed in the army afterward because he had no home, no friends and knew no other place to go. But he, too, had long been dabbling in political ideas which, in a half-educated way, he had picked up from newspapers; like the others, he hated the republic and the Socialists and the Jews; he had been going to the beer-hall meetings and even finding that he could speak at them with effect; and he had been dreaming dreams of a mighty, united Germany and of himself as leader of the vast popular movement that would bring it about. The gas lamp flared over the table and the beer-mugs. This "party" they were asking him to join was a ridiculous affair; but suddenly the corporal agreed. He received membership card No. 7. His name was Adolf Hitler, and the party was to become the National Socialist—or Nazi—party, that fifteen years later was to conquer Germany.

Corporal Hitler went back to his barracks, and the great world knew nothing of him. But it was soon to be hearing a good deal about another World War corporal who had fought on the opposite side, in the Italian army. Italy had been one of the victor powers, but in her great cities there was almost as much unrest and dissatisfaction and disappointment and violence as in the defeated countries. The Italians felt that they had been badly treated at the Peace Conference, where they had been denied certain gains of territory and colonies which they had been promised and to which they believed themselves entitled. The Communists were attracting many industrial workers; prices were high and wages were low; there were strikes and riots; and the democratic leaders came and went in Parliament, without strong support behind them, doing little that was effective, while the government slid toward bankruptcy and the parties quarreled bitterly. Through this turmoil there was rising the figure of Benito Mussolini—another strange man, very different from the unknown German soldier, yet in some ways curiously like him.

Mussolini was the son of a blacksmith. Like Hitler,

he had had a lonely, unhappy and poverty-stricken childhood; but where the German took it out in dreams of art and politics, the Italian took it out in wildness, surliness and pugnacity. He never could hold a job. He was always in fights. He was naturally a rebel; and he learned radical politics from his father, a village anarchist who had named his son after Benito Juarez, the great Mexican revolutionary leader. He became active in the local socialist movement; and as a young man he fled to Switzerland to avoid doing his military service. There he slept under bridges, worked fitfully as a day laborer and got into trouble with the police. But there he also fell in with the strange group of international revolutionaries and radical agitators who in the years before the Great War gathered in that small country to find sanctuary from their own governments. They were poor exiles of no position in the great world, but often of high idealism and intellectual powers; they lived cheaply in furnished rooms, studying and preaching Marx and the other revolutionary philosophers; they held meetings and they corresponded endlessly with radical movements all over Europe. Among them, Mussolini is supposed to have met Lenin; and he did fall under the influence of one of Lenin's colleagues, a brilliant Russian woman who took the wild youth, helped and steadied him, educated him and finally sent him back to Italy a flaming revolutionary socialist with a command of oratory and considerable ability as a writer.

Hitler, when the war began, was an utterly obscure casual laborer and postcard artist in Munich. But Mussolini was already well known in Italy. He had made himself one of the recognized leaders of the Italian Socialist party and was the editor of its chief paper. The Socialists opposed Italy's entrance into the war. But Mussolini—restless, vigorous, ambitious and enticed by money from the French government —suddenly switched over to urge that Italy should go in. The party expelled him; he merely founded his own paper, the *Popolo d'Italia*, and in blazing editorials continued to preach war. Italy entered the struggle. Mussolini fought for a time as a common soldier, but was wounded after a few months, and returned to his editorial desk in Milan. He was still a socialist and his ideas were radical and revolutionary, but he had betrayed the party and was no longer a member of it. Amid all the turmoil and unrest of Italy just after the war he was looking about for some place which he could make for himself. Mussolini had an idea. In 1919, just about the time that Hitler and his acquaintances were sitting around their beermugs in Munich, in the offices of the *Popolo d'Italia* in Milan the radical editor was forming the first detachment of Fascist Blackshirts.

They were unemployed ex-soldiers, most of them, restless and violent young men who liked the idea of putting on black-shirt uniforms, swaggering with clubs and revolvers about the streets and believing that they were fighting for something grand and

noble—though just what, they did not quite know.
There were thousands like them in Italy, as in all the
other countries coming out of the war, and the movement rapidly spread. Like Hitler's friends in Germany, the Fascisti, as they called themselves, did not
know what they wanted. But probably Mussolini
did. He saw himself becoming the head of an organization that was at the same time a political party
which could vote him into power and a kind of private army or gang that could beat up opponents, riot
in the streets and seize control where they were not
strong enough to achieve it in the ordinary way.
Mussolini wanted power. "We, the survivors who
have returned," he declared, "demand the right of
governing Italy."

As to how he would govern it, he was not so sure.
It the latter part of 1920 there was a series of great
strikes in Italy. The owners tried to shut the men out
of the factories; the men in response tried to take
possession of them and operate them on their own
account. Mussolini had himself encouraged exactly
this kind of tactics in an earlier strike and had been
called "the Lenin of Italy" for it by one of his en-
thusiastic friends; and he did not oppose the seizure
of the factories in 1920. In the end the whole thing
was settled by the government and normal work was
resumed. But it caused great excitement. The sight
of red flags flying over some of the biggest Italian
industrial plants, while the machinery turned within,
operated by workers who had put their managers

and owners into the streets, and while armed patrols of workers went by outside, sometimes shouting for revolution, left a deep impression upon all those who feared that Europe was about to be swallowed in a vast wave of Bolshevism from Russia. Although the occupation of the factories was ended, labor troubles continued, and more and more Mussolini saw his opportunity. The wealthy people in Italy were terrified by fear of revolution; the business men wanted an end of strikes and unrest and demands for high wages, while great numbers of middle-class Italians and even workpeople were growing tired of the turmoil and confusion. They were tired of liberal and radical ideas which seemed to lead to nothing but trouble, they were tired of the old political parties which seemed only to squabble helplessly with each other, they were tired of Communist and "red" agitation. Among great numbers of Italians—including many of those who had wealth and influence—there was a general reaction against all these things, and Mussolini's Blackshirts made themselves the center of the movement.

He was already at war with the Socialists, who had expelled him, and when the appearance of Communist administrations in some of the northern cities led to violence and disturbance, Mussolini turned loose his Fascist gangs to slug and shoot the Communists out of office and take it for themselves. Not many think now that there was ever any great danger of Italy's going Bolshevist. But Mussolini, the one-

time revolutionary, declared a kind of guerrilla war
on "reds" and radicals everywhere. His Blackshirt
squads roamed the country, terrorizing Socialist and
Communist leaders, beating them, administering huge
doses of castor oil to them, breaking up strikes, smashing or even burning down Socialist and Communist
headquarters. They marched in military formation,
compelling everyone to uncover as they passed; they
dashed about in military trucks; they pretended to
police the country, even to regulate prices; everywhere they declared that they would restore order
and actually kept the country almost in a state of
civil war. Bankers and industrialists helped to support
and arm them; the army and the police seldom interfered. By the latter part of 1921 they had a large
group of their own deputies in Parliament, and Mussolini's private army and political party had become
almost a recognized institution of the state.

Still Mussolini did not know just how he would
use it. He seems to have felt that the violence was
going too far and to have been unwilling to cut himself off from all support from the great mass of working people, whom once he had led. Suddenly he made
a "peace treaty" with the Socialists and labor unions,
agreeing to end "all menaces, all reprisals, all punish-
ments, all vengeances, all personal violence." But he
had started a storm which he could not stop. Many
of the Fascisti paid no attention to the peace treaty,
and when he denounced them as "hot-heads" they
began to attack him as a traitor. There was a Fascist

riot in Modena, in which seven people were killed. Mussolini resigned from the Fascist party. The party went on without him, supported by the army, the industrialists, the landowners, and by the fact that a great many men by this time were finding their careers in its activities. Mussolini withdrew his resignation. Carried along by his own army, he now turned it not only against the radicals and labor unions, but against the parliamentary government itself. The Fascists would overthrow democracy and seize power.

Italy was recovering by this time from the effects of the war, but its democratic government was weak, its financial affairs were in bad shape, there was little strength or ability among the old political leaders and few had any confidence in them. The Fascisti did not believe in democracy. They thought it wasteful and corrupt and incompetent. They were themselves a military organization; they had accepted Mussolini as their "Duce," or absolute leader; they were content to take orders from him and his lieutenants and they dreamed of a whole nation which should do the same. It would be a strong, glorious, warlike Italy, marching all together to prosperity and great things. All the political bickerings and party fights would be swept away; the old men who had held power too long would be replaced by the young veterans of the war, and all would work together under the firm, efficient hand of a single dictator.

In October, 1922, there was a great Fascist party

congress in Naples. Forty thousand Blackshirts paraded in military formation through the streets, and Mussolini made flaming speeches. The time had come. The nation had to be saved from its democratic politicians. Liberalism had finished its task and should be done away with; it was time to call in "all the forces of the new generation which has emerged from the war and the victory." His followers responded with enthusiasm as he poured out the oratory. "Either the government will be given to us," he thundered, "or we shall seize it by marching on Rome!" The crowds roared back: "To Rome! To Rome!" Mussolini and his Fascists had proclaimed a revolution.

But he did not go to Rome at once. He went back to his newspaper office at Milan. Meanwhile, various high officers of the army had apparently agreed with him that the time had come to put a Fascist government in power, or at least let him know that the army would not interfere with the rather curious kind of revolution which was actually being planned. On October 26, a group of leading Fascists in Rome demanded that the government should be placed in the Fascists' hands. The Premier, Facta, immediately resigned. In Rome there was no great excitement; governments were always resigning, and the Fascists were always making trouble. But next day people heard that Mussolini had ordered his Blackshirt armies to march upon the capital. There were supposed to be something like 800,000 of them in the country, while trainloads of them were now rolling northward from Naples, packed with the delegates from the congress. Newspaper men began to ask themselves whether it really was a revolution, and big headlines began to appear all over the world.

Presently Fascist circulars were appearing: "We march to Rome to give Italy her full liberty. . . . Marching with the sincere desire of peace and love, our greatest shout shall always be: Long live the army, long live the King and long live Italy!" If the Fascists were not marching on Rome, some of them, at any rate, were coming by trains, buses and wagons and beginning to gather outside the city. On the morning of the 28th, people in the capital began to hear about barbed-wire barricades being set up at the entrances to the city and about cavalry and machine guns being put in position; the newspapers did not appear and the telephone and telegraph seemed to have broken down. At noon it was announced that martial law had been proclaimed, and it looked as though the government might act firmly to scatter the rather ragged groups of young men who were collecting to threaten it; but then two hours later the proclamation was withdrawn. The King of Italy had refused to sign it, perhaps because he was afraid of bloodshed, perhaps because he was afraid the army might not obey if ordered to fire on the Fascists.

The politicians were trying to form a new government in which Mussolini would have a part; a few Fascists were demonstrating mildly in the city; it was reported that the Fascists were seizing the city

governments in the north, with the police and soldiers standing by as they did so, but nothing much
seemed to be happening. In Milan, however, there
was a stirring scene. Mussolini's editors and em-
ployees were throwing up barricades in front of the
offices of his *Popolo d'Italia*, mounting machine guns
and getting ready for the enemy (though none was
in sight) while the great man waited in his office for
word from Rome. Suddenly thinking that he heard
trouble, the leader snatched up his loaded rifle and
dashed downstairs to the barricade; as he climbed it,
there was the crack of another rifle and a bullet
whizzed through his hair just above the ear, grazing
his skull. It was one of his own excited followers
who, coming just behind him, had opened fire upon
the supposed enemy with the best of intentions but
a bad aim; and thus it was only by a tiny fraction of
an inch that Mussolini missed being the first, and almost the only, victim of his own revolution. He went
back to his office.

About midday on the 29th there came a message
from the King, offering to make Mussolini Premier
of Italy. He went off that night, through cheering
crowds in the streets and at the station, to make his
own "march" on Rome in the sleeping car of a special train. In Rome next morning there were more
cheers and flowers at the station. "Friends," said
Mussolini, "his majesty the King has called me to
Rome to form a government. I will form it. But I
demand calm, order, discipline. . . ." He went on

to see the King. Meanwhile, the Fascists who had gathered outside the city were let in. Nobody knows how many of them there were—probably no more than eight or ten thousand, who could have been easily scattered by a few regiments—but now that it was all over many thousands more poured into the city, countless people in Rome put on their black shirts, and it was a huge parade which the King and Mussolini reviewed next day. Almost immediately, however, this triumphant Fascist host began to make a nuisance of itself with various riots and disorders, and next day Mussolini ordered them out.

The famous "march on Rome" was pretty much of a comic-opera affair. There really was no revolution. The army, the industrialists, the wealthy and conservative people and the King appear to have decided among them that it would be better, after all the disturbance which his Fascisti had caused, to let Mussolini take over the government. It was still a parliamentary government. In a way there seemed to be little change. But it was the beginning of the end of democracy in Italy, and the end was to come quickly. By careful but fairly rapid steps Mussolini was to make himself an absolute dictator over this country, developing a form of completely autocratic, militaristic and irresponsible government which was new to Western Europe. And Italy was one of the three or four greatest European nations. This was a kind of solution for the problems of the post-war un-

rest on which the authors of the peace treaties had
never calculated.

In other ways, meanwhile, the Continent was being
put back together again. The League of Nations was
set up in Geneva, and one of its first and most important works was to raise and administer the big
international loans which rescued the new governments of Austria and Hungary from their appalling
financial difficulties, set those fragments of a once
great empire going again and gave them and their
peoples some chance of life. Germany had been completely disarmed. Nothing had been done about disarming the victor powers, and these had their doubts
about the ability of the League to keep the peace in
the future; but they were themselves combining together into groups for each other's support in a way
that seemed to promise some order and security in
the tangled new world. Czechoslovakia, Rumania and
Yugoslavia formed the "Little Entente," which en-
closed Hungary like a vise and was intended to make
sure that she would never try to regain the territories
which the others had acquired from her under the
peace settlements. France entered into alliances with
Poland and with the Little Entente in order to support these countries as a wall against Bolshevist Russia and as a ring which would threaten Germany in
case the latter should ever again attempt an attack
on France. Economic life was in general beginning
to revive. But there was one problem for which no

answer had been found. It was the problem of Germany's unsettled reparations debt.

Since the signing of the peace treaty, the diplomats and politicians had been roaming around Europe from one international conference to another, trying to decide how much Germany could pay, trying to decide how the victors would divide up the payments among themselves, trying to decide what they should do about the enormous debts which the Allies owed each other and which all of them owed the United States as a result of the war-time borrowing. In May, 1921, the Allies' Reparations Commission finally fixed the total bill for which Germany would be responsible at the colossal sum of $33,000,000,000, and in an ultimatum gave the German government six days in which officially to accept the obligation. But even this was an "outside" figure; and there was still a good deal of uncertainty as to how much of it would ever be paid off, and how fast. To begin with, Germany was required to pay over to the Allies $500,000,000 a year in cash and large additional sums in goods, particularly coal and building materials for the reconstruction of the devastated areas in France. The payments were never made in full, or anything like it. Germany could not or would not find the money, and the Reparations Commission soon had to reduce the cash payments, until in August, 1922, it suspended them altogether for six months. There was constant trouble with the deliveries of goods. And though German industry was again operating well

enough, German government finances in the meanwhile began to go from bad to worse.

To pay the Allies, the German government not
only had to raise the money, in German paper marks,
from its own people; it then had to buy gold or foreign money with these marks, in order to "transfer"
the payment to the Allies in a form in which they
could use it. But the more marks it offered for this
purpose, the cheaper they became, the less foreign
money could be bought with them, and the more it
looked as if the whole German economic system was
going to smash. By the end of 1922, the German
mark, which had been worth about twenty-four
cents before the war, was worth much less than one-
fiftieth of a cent. Where it had taken only four marks
to buy a dollar before the war, it now took over
seven thousand. Faced with all this, the Allies fell
into a serious dispute among themselves. The British
(who found, among other things, that the German
payments in goods were competing with their own
exports) argued that the results proved that Germany simply could not pay reparations in the
amounts demanded of her and that the whole scheme
of payments would have to be revised and reduced
if Germany was not to go into a complete collapse.
The French, led by their Premier, Poincaré—a rigid,
flinty, rather narrow-minded but intensely energetic
little man—insisted on the letter of the treaties.

The reparations payments, they held, were not the
only reason why German finances were tottering.

Germany had paid much of the cost of the Great War by borrowing from her people instead of by taxing them, and now had an enormous domestic debt left over which she was finding it difficult or impossible to pay. Instead of trying to meet these and other costs of her own government, as well as reparations, by heavy taxation, she was simply printing money. The French insisted that Germany was not unable to pay reparations, but merely unwilling to do so; the Germans were deliberately refusing to impose taxation, to put their finances in order, to make the sacrifices necessary. They would have to be compelled to change their policy. The French declared that they would send their armies into the Ruhr—Germany's great industrial district, lying just over the border, where most of her richest coal mines were and where some of her largest plants, including the huge Krupp steel works, were concentrated—to seize and hold the area until Germany should show a willingness to live up to her obligations.

In the first days of January, 1923, there was a tense meeting of the Allied statesmen in Paris; some people thought it was the most serious crisis since 1914, and perhaps, considering all that was to happen afterward, they were right. There was no agreement. The British solemnly declared that Poincaré's plan would not only fail to produce reparation payments but would probably "have a grave and disastrous effect upon the economic situation in Europe," and the British would therefore have nothing to do with it.

Poincaré curtly answered that the British suggestions for lightening the load on Germany would mean "considerable reduction in the debt owing to France and the overthrow of the Treaty of Versailles, and that it is impossible to accept such propositions." The conference broke up; a day or two later the Reparations Commission formally declared that Germany had wilfully defaulted, and the winter dawn of January 11 saw long columns of French troops marching down the roads to Essen, the chief city of the Ruhr.

The advance guards reached the city a little after noon; the few German sentries simply standing aside to let them pass, for they could do nothing else. By evening the French had seized the post office, the railway station, the mayor's office, and were commandeering hotels and schools for quarters; their machine guns were set up everywhere, and French uniforms seemed to fill the city. The sidewalk crowds watched them come, sullenly and in silence; there was no violence, but none could miss the intense hatred with which this beaten people watched the invasion of conquerors whom they were helpless to resist. The government in Berlin, strongly under the influence of the great industrial magnates of the Ruhr, announced that it would pay no more reparations of any kind; it had no means of preventing the French occupation, but it resolved upon a passive resistance in every way possible to the French demands, and it set the following Sunday as a great day of national mourning for the German people.

Probably the British and the French were each partly right about the Germans; it was tragic that neither could accept the other's policy. If the French had agreed to the British plan for reducing the debt, the whole matter could have been settled more easily and France would probably have got much more money than she did in the end. If the British had stood firmly behind the French, the Germans would not have been encouraged to resist and again the matter might have found a better settlement. And other things might not have happened. The workers of the German trades unions and their powerful Social Democratic party suspected the industrialists who were in control of the government and who were urging resistance. The Social Democrats accused them of simply trying to stir up hatred in order to avoid paying their share of taxes for reparations, and argued for an attempt, instead, to work for international understanding. If the British had not encouraged the industrial magnates, the Social Democrats might perhaps have put them out of office, and not only found some solution for the reparations question but also have established the progressive and democratic parties in firm control in Germany. As it was, the people were too bitter; the Social Democrats were afraid of seeming to yield to the French, and all they did was to tell their followers to gather in their own halls on the coming Sunday instead of joining in the outdoor demonstrations of mourning.

In Berlin that Sunday there were some curious

scenes. Perhaps 100,000 people—the followers of the
conservative and middle-class parties—flocked into
the open space before the Reichstag building to make
their protest against the Ruhr seizure. Yet it was not
a large crowd for such an occasion in Germany, since
the trades unionists had stayed away. The demon-
strators sang patriotic songs for a time and listened to
speeches; but they were very quiet about it and broke
up and went home in an orderly way. Not far off,
however, there was a smaller and very different
demonstration. There was a mob before the French
Embassy, yelling itself hoarse, singing and trying to
break through into the building. Presently the
mounted police and soldiers arrived and scattered
them, but a part broke away and made a dash for the
Hotel Bellevue, where the Allied commission super-
vising German disarmament had its headquarters.
They smashed through the doors, but the police were
there, too, and they got no farther. As they finally
trailed away onlookers noticed that they were young
men, most of them, students, former soldiers, belonging to the extreme reactionary elements who hated
the republic and all its works, and they were commanded by followers, as one newspaper report said,
"of the reactionary Bavarian leader, Hitler." The
unknown infantry corporal who had joined the six-
man "party" in Munich three and a half years before
had come a good way since then, and in the chaotic
months to follow he was to go a good way farther.

The Ruhr occupation divided France and Great

Britain and so made any strong control over the affairs of Europe even less possible than before. Within Germany at the same time it weakened the democratic parties and supporters of the republic, who left the resistance to others, and strengthened every sort of extremism—the Communists, the monarchists, the old army leaders, the violent and embittered Nationalists, and the small but growing National Socialist party of Adolf Hitler. And it led to a dreadful summer in Germany—the famous summer of inflation.

Some believe that the inflation was the unavoidable result of the Ruhr occupation coming on top of all the dislocations and disturbances that had gone before; some believe that it was deliberately set in motion by the great industrialists in order to escape reparations payments, in order to wipe out all the debts left over from the war, in order to ruin the costly industrial pension systems, in order to break the middle-class and salaried workers, to clean the slate and enable Germany to start over again under conditions which would give the advantage to the great industries and banks. Again, perhaps there is some truth in both arguments. At any rate, the government, which had already been printing money for its expenses, found itself printing more and more as it tried to shut down the Ruhr coal mines, to feed the Ruhr population thus thrown out of work, to meet the other costs which the disruption of German economy involved, and to keep pace with prices which were now rising very fast. A dollar had bought about

7,000 paper marks when the French entered the Ruhr; it bought about 15,000 before January was half over; it bought about 80,000 paper marks by the beginning of June and 150,000 a couple of weeks later. And then the value of the mark really began to go, until, when the old mark was finally done away with, its value was officially set at 4,200,000,-000,000 to the dollar.

All that summer and fall people stood in long lines at groceries and shops, desperately trying to spend all the money they had, every pfennig they had just received in their pay envelopes, before it should become worthless. Prices were marked up hour by hour. A housewife with enough money to buy a loaf of bread one day would find the same loaf costing ten times as much on the day after. The printing presses could not turn out new money fast enough, so old bills were simply printed over with longer and longer strings of zeros after the figure. Salaries and wages went up, of course, as the value of the mark went down, but not so fast; and while the people stood in their lines waiting to spend their vanishing money they knew that their savings and "fixed incomes" of every sort—such as pensions, insurance payments, interest on war loans and industrial bonds, anything required to be paid them in a stated amount of marks—were disappearing into thin air. It was a terrible experience for millions of Germans, especially millions of middle-class Germans—small salaried people, officials and shopkeepers—who had always tried to save their money and look out for themselves and make a position in their world, and who now found themselves utterly ruined.

It was not only tragic; it was unsettling. Everything seemed to be going to pieces. When a workman found himself paying five hundred billion marks (which once would have been the same as a hundred billion dollars) for a single street-car ride, he simply lost all count of money and everything else. Germany was full of ruined, angry, uncertain people; nobody knew what was going to happen and many ceased to care what they did. There were great demonstrations, strikes and street riots, in some of which dozens of people were killed. The Communists seemed to be growing rapidly in strength, and in August they attempted a general strike in Berlin. But in Bavaria a week or two later there was another kind of demonstration. In a huge review, marching hosts of nationalists, monarchists, conservative parties and fighting associations passed in military formation. One leader was General Erich Ludendorff; he was already rather more than half mad, but every German knew him as the military genius who had directed all the German armies during the last years of the Great War. The other was the former corporal, Adolf Hitler.

His party, which had begun with seven regular members in 1919, now had 70,000, with many more who flocked to his meetings and listened to his furious oratory. He was calling for revolution, bloodshed and dictatorship; he was screaming against the republican government, which he declared to be a creation of Jews, radicals and traitors; and he was shouting in particular for a march on "Red Berlin" to clean out that "pigsty" of Communism. Other powerful people, who wanted to put down radical agitation, who wanted to separate Bavaria from the rest of Germany or bring back the former Bavarian king, were encouraging him and giving him money. He now had his followers armed and in uniform, the beginning of another private political army like Mussolini's Fascists. Kahr, the governor of Bavaria, Lossow, the regular general commanding the army units there, and Seisser, the chief of the Munich police, seem to have entered into some kind of revolutionary plot with Ludendorff and Hitler; and the authorities in Berlin began to be afraid that a civil war among Communists, reactionaries and republicans was about to break out.

Something had to be done. In September the government at last turned seriously to the task of ending the inflation and establishing a new money to replace the wreckage of the old. At the same time, the Germans began to abandon their passive resistance to the French in the Ruhr, while the Allies on their side began to look about for some better answer to the whole reparations question. But Hitler was inflamed with his idea of a revolution and a march upon Berlin, and had picked November 9, the anniversary of the founding of the republican government which he hated, as the day for it. In Munich on the evening of November 8 there was a great meeting of the nationalists and monarchists in the Bürgerbräu beer-hall. The three high Bavarian officials, Kahr, Lossow and Seisser, did not believe the time for revolution had come, but they were at the meeting, and Kahr was halfway through a speech denouncing the republic when there was a commotion at the door. Hitler, surrounded by a squad of his uniformed storm troopers, forced his way into the center of the hall; there he sprang suddenly to a table, drew a revolver and fired two shots into the ceiling.

In the astonished silence he shouted that the revolution had broken out, that the army and police were with him, that the governments of Bavaria and of Germany had been overthrown, and that no one could leave the hall, which was already surrounded by his armed troopers. Then he jumped down, hurried the three officials away with him into a side room and begged and pleaded with them to join him and see the adventure through. He offered them high posts in the new government, of which he would be the head. "He wept with excitement and ordered a stein of beer. Suddenly Ludendorff appeared in medals and uniform and urged them to accept." They did accept—or pretended to; they all went back to the main hall and poured out a torrent of speech-making. Then the officials went home, leaving Hitler and his followers sitting in the Bürgerbräu while his storm-trooper detachments ranged through the streets of Munich, creating a wild disorder, attacking Jews and radicals, smashing into trade-union headquarters and republican newspaper offices and trying to capture the railway station and post office.

But the police held the buildings against the storm troopers, for the police were not on Hitler's side. He sent messengers off after Kahr and the others, but got no reply. Finally, at three o'clock in the morning word came to him that Kahr and the rest had gone back on their undertaking. They had, they said, only pretended to accept because Hitler had been threatening them with his revolver; and they would have nothing more to do with him. The police and army were already scattering the storm troopers and restoring order in the city. Hitler could not fight such forces; the whole thing was a ridiculous failure, and there was nothing he could do except order a parade for next morning. He thought he might still be able to rouse the people; but when the marching columns set out next day, with their brown uniforms, with their swastika flags in great blood-red splashes above the line, with their cheers and songs, they only found the police and army troops everywhere, watching them in silence. The procession wound on toward the main square; as the leading files approached, they saw the police and soldiery drawn up. Hitler did not believe that the army would actually fire upon his patriotic youths and ex-soldiers, and the column moved on. But suddenly there was a loud crackle of rifle shots; a flag went down; men were lying in the street and the Nazi marchers were scattering. General Ludendorff alone in his full uniform marched straight up to the troops; they opened and let him pass. Hitler was on the pavement; he had fallen or been pulled down and had broken his shoulder. Eighteen of his followers were lying dead; others were wounded; the rest were running, and as the sharp smell of powder smoke drifted away through the street, the "beer-hall putsch," as it has ever since been called, was over.

In the excitement Hitler was smuggled away, but he was found a few days later, tried and given a short sentence of imprisonment. The Nazi party was ordered to disband; its storm troopers put away their uniforms, its chief newspaper was suppressed and with its leader in jail the whole movement seemed to be at an end. Still, 1,900,000 Germans voted for Nazi candidates at the parliamentary election the following spring, and thirty-two Nazi representatives took their seats in the Reichstag. But the worst of the troubles which lay behind all this mood of wild reaction and violence were coming to an end. The government had set up the new money; it could not help the countless people who had already been ruined, and the old billion and trillion mark bills still were seen, but the uncertainty was over and the inflation stopped. At the same time the Allies had appointed a commission, not of diplomats or politicians, but of business experts and economists, to study the whole problem of reparations. With an American, Charles

G. Dawes, at their head, they set themselves to find out, not how much Germany ought to pay, but how much as a practical matter she could pay. They worked all through the first months of 1924, finally producing a definite plan which everyone, including the Germans, agreed to as fair and reasonable.

This "Dawes Plan," as it was called, did not attempt to fix the final amount which Germany should ultimately pay; it did find that the most she could provide, once her industry had been set going again and her money troubles brought to an end, would be about $620,000,000 a year. This was much less than the French had been trying to collect when they marched into the Ruhr; while the Dawes Plan held that Germany could not pay even this much for another five years. For the first year of the plan, Germany was to pay only $250,000,000, and most of that she was to get by borrowing from the Allied countries and the United States. Thus the final outcome of the occupation of the Ruhr was a great reduction in the German debt. But the French accepted the situation, and the Germans went honestly to work to pay the lowered bill. The plan went into effect on September 1, 1924; at the same time, the French marched out of the Ruhr, and the violence of both the Communists and the Nationalists died away in Germany. In December, 1924, there was another election, and Hitler's Nazis got only 900,000 votes— less than half of what they had received in the spring —and only fourteen seats in the Reichstag.

It began to seem as though the dark clouds of the war were rolling away at last. The problem of reparations, most people thought, had finally been settled. There had been no great Bolshevist revolution in Western Europe; even the Russians had laid aside a good many of their Communist ideas for the time being, and the other powers were glad to leave them alone to work out their own problems. Most of the border disputes had been settled, not always with justice, but with what seemed to be finality. Everywhere people were at work again, and fairly prosperous. One serious problem did remain. Thinking of the future, no one, not even the victorious powers, felt too safe. Germany had been compelled to disarm; but the huge French army and powerful British fleet remained, each costing their peoples enormous sums, while the smaller states were all arming themselves as rapidly as they could afford to do so. No one really seemed to believe that war had been done away with—and might not another war some day come?

Here, however, there was the League of Nations, pledged to defend every member against an attack from any side, with its great offices in Geneva now actively at work, with its organization perfected and with its appearance of being at the beginning of great things. It was busy on disarmament; it had actually settled several minor disputes; it had arranged the loans which had saved Austria and Hungary from complete collapse. Would not the League guarantee the peace of Europe? Unfortunately, in the same summer which had seen the inflation wreck in Germany, something rather disturbing had happened in the Mediterranean.

Mussolini now ruled in Italy as dictator, and one of the first aims of his "strong" foreign policy had been to establish Italian control over Albania—the small mountain country just across the Adriatic Sea from Southern Italy. On August 27, 1923, an Italian general who was at work laying out the boundary between Albania and Greece was assassinated. Mussolini had no proof that Greeks were responsible, or even that the murder had taken place on the Greek side of the boundary. But perhaps he felt that he needed some stirring, exciting incident to prove that his new government was building the powerful, military and glorious Italy which it had promised. Instantly he sent a twenty-four-hour ultimatum to Greece demanding apologies, demanding punishment for the murderers and demanding an indemnity of 50,000,000 lire. The Greeks were willing to apologize, but asked for a conference about the indemnity. Mussolini responded by mobilizing the Italian fleet; and on the afternoon of August 31 the governor of the Greek island of Corfu was astonished by the arrival of an Italian naval officer, who told him that the island was about to be bombarded and captured. The governor explained that one of the two ancient forts on the island was occupied by a lot of refugees and orphans, the other by a police school; he had no troops or guns and no way of resisting. But the

Italians had to have their bombardment all the same. The ships opened fire on the forts, managing to kill fifteen or twenty of the refugees and wreck the study of the head of the police school; and with that the Italians landed and seized the island. Greece at once appealed to the League of Nations.

This seemed a plain case of outrageous violence which the League should immediately have stepped in to reprove and punish. But Mussolini announced that Italy did "not like the League of Nations. We respect its aims, but I completely deny its authority to intervene in a matter affecting Italian honor." If the League meddled into the affair, he would resign from the League. Italy was a major power; and in this rather serious test of its authority, the League hesitated. In the end a way out was found by turning over the question to another international body, the Council of Ambassadors, which was not a part of the League, and the council decided that Greece should pay the indemnity on condition that the Italians got out of Corfu. So it was settled. This, many people said, proved the power of the League, for it had prevented a war and compelled Mussolini to give up the island. But there were others who did not believe that Mussolini had ever intended to keep Corfu, who thought the League had shirked its duty under Mussolini's threats by turning the affair over to the Council of Ambassadors, and who did not see much justice in the settlement anyway. And they began to wonder how well the League of Nations was really going to

work as a means of keeping the peace in Europe and
guaranteeing the safety of its peoples.

But even for this problem there seemed to be the
beginnings of a solution. For one thing, new men
were coming into power in the big nations, and new
and more generous ideas, not so deeply colored by
the bitterness of the war, were becoming popular. In
1924 the first Labor Party government came to power
in Great Britain, with Ramsay MacDonald as Prime
Minister—a pacifist, a liberal and a believer in international understanding. It did not last long, but it left
its influence behind it. In France, the government of
Poincaré, the narrow-minded, conservative leader of
the war years, was replaced by a liberal, democratic,
"Left" government, with Aristide Briand, a sincere
believer in peace, as its foreign minister. And the foreign minister of Germany was now Gustav Stresemann, another remarkable statesman, who had decided that the best way in which his country could
win back her place as a great and independent power
was by fulfilling her treaty obligations, and working
with the Allies rather than fighting against them.

In the autumn of 1925 Briand and Stresemann met
with British and Italian representatives at Locarno,
on the lovely Lake Maggiore under the Swiss Alps,
to make a new European agreement. They could not
deal with all the possible causes of war, but they did
deal with what seemed one of the greatest. Germany,
France and Belgium agreed to maintain the boundaries between them, including the demilitarized area

along the Rhine, as laid down in the Versailles treaty,* and promised never to wage war over that frontier. But more than that, Great Britain and Italy guaranteed the agreement; they promised, that is, not only to help France and Belgium if Germany should violate the treaty and attack them, but to help Germany in case France should violate her word. It meant that for the first time since the Great War, Germany was treated as an equal by the victorious powers. In return Germany signed arbitration treaties with her neighbors, and agreed not to object to treaties which France signed with Czechoslovakia and Poland, in which those nations promised to give each other immediate help in case any one of them should be attacked by Germany. Finally, the Allies invited Germany to join the League of Nations, as an equal member and of her own free will.

Here at last, it seemed, was an answer even to the problem of "security," or safety against war. Germany was again received as an independent great power into the common society of nations. With the British and Italian guarantees of the Locarno treaty, there was no longer reason for Germany to fear an attack by France or France to fear another invasion by the Germans; and one need worry no longer about the Franco-German border, over which so many wars had been fought. As to Germany's eastern frontier, matters were not so certain, but the French treaties with Poland and Czechoslovakia, which Germany

* See page 10.

accepted, seemed to make that part of the world reasonably safe as well. With this, all the worst problems left over from the war had apparently been settled. Everywhere there was a general feeling of friendliness, and people began to talk about the "spirit of Locarno," in which most of the old hatreds and fears seemed to have disappeared. It was seven years since the guns had fallen silent on the Western Front. But the new Europe had apparently been put together at last.

3. GAPS IN THE DEFENSES

YET IT WAS BY NO MEANS THE KIND OF new Europe which the authors of the peace treaties had intended to build; and it was to last for barely five years. Although very great problems had been settled, there were many things that were wrong about the settlements. But most people did not see this at the time. The five years from 1925 to 1930 were on the whole good years for Europe. Its peoples were busy and fairly prosperous. They paid more attention to their domestic affairs than to quarrels with other countries. In most of the great nations the war-time leaders had died or grown old and retired; and their places had been taken either by men like Briand and Stresemann, who were believers in peace and international friendship, or else by the new leaders, like Mussolini, who were too busy, setting their new governments in order, to cause trouble elsewhere.

In Russia, Lenin, the great father of the Bolshevist revolution, had died. A silent, rather mysterious person called Stalin had taken Lenin's place, and was making himself the absolute master of the whole vast country. The rest of the world knew very little about him. But it saw him drive Trotsky, the second great leader of the revolution, out of power and finally into exile, because Trotsky was too radical and still believed in spreading Bolshevism throughout the world. It saw Stalin invite foreign engineers and business men into Russia to help build up the country's industries, and watched him send out his ambassadors and trade representatives to buy the machinery and materials which he needed for this from the "capitalistic" countries. And in 1928 it saw him begin the great "Five Year Plan" which was to make Russia over and provide her with the factories and power houses and railways and raw materials that would raise the Russian people from their desperate poverty. Plainly, it seemed that Russia was far too much occupied with her own affairs to be a threat to anyone else; the rest of the world lost its fear of Bolshevist revolution and began to think that trade with Russia might grow into an important help toward prosperity for the whole world.

At Geneva, the League of Nations met regularly, busying itself with all kinds of questions, large and small. The leading statesmen of Europe were often to be found at its meetings, along with scores of lesser people—diplomats from the smaller countries, students of international affairs, the many secretaries and officials of the League itself, drawn from many countries, and newspaper men from all over the world. These people met and mingled with each other in the council rooms and corridors of the League buildings, in the Geneva restaurants and bars; they felt that they were at a great center of international activity and co-operation, and to many of them it seemed as though a real international organization—more interested in the welfare of the world as a whole than in the greeds and fears and jealousies of the different nations—was growing up. They talked about the "Geneva atmosphere," just as they had talked about the "Locarno spirit."

It was true that the greeds and fears of the different nations were always there and always came out strongly whenever some really important question appeared. It was true that the League always seemed to spend much more of its time in making speeches and in deciding to investigate problems than it did in actually settling them. People could not forget things like Mussolini's bombardment of Corfu and other affairs of the sort in which the League's action had seemed rather feeble. It was realized that there were a lot of "gaps" in the League's defenses against war, and that there would have to be new treaties and understandings to strengthen these weak spots before the nations would really feel safe in the League's protection. But many earnest men thought that it would not be too hard to devise such additional treaties, and went to work quite seriously to produce them. Once the right system had been discovered and the nations had agreed to accept it, they thought, the League would surely grow into a great power, greater than all the quarreling national states, and able to force them to keep the peace in the interests of the world as a whole. It was surely just a matter of finding the right words—the right "formula," as they called it—and everything would turn out all right, nations would be peaceful and friendly and prosperous and considerate of each other, the great problems would be solved and a good world would come out of it all.

Many intelligent men really thought so in those years, and perhaps it is conceivable that something of the kind might have happened. The reasons why it did not are many and complicated, and the rest of this book will be devoted to showing them at work. What seems the one broadest reason was the ultimate rise in Germany of an extreme, savage and warlike government, resolved to break up by force the whole arrangement worked out by the victor powers at Versailles, and incapable of proposing any other arrangement of Europe to which the other powers could feel that they might safely agree. But there were many reasons, of course, behind the rise of the German Nazis; the mistakes, stupidities and selfishnesses of other peoples played their part; no one can ever finally say just what "caused" anything in history or who was most responsible, for that is something on which everyone must make up his own mind for himself in the end.

All that can be said is that there was a great deal in this new Europe that was good and that might have been the beginning for a still better way of carrying on the affairs of mankind. But there was a great deal in it, too, that was dangerous. President Wilson and the other statesmen who had invented the League of Nations thought of it as an association of free and democratic peoples. At home these peoples would govern themselves by the machinery of elections and parliaments and free discussion, and that would make it easier for them to govern the world through a league that was really a kind of parliament of nations, with the same kind of electoral machinery and relying in the same way on public discussion and public opinion. But this new Europe that appeared after 1925 was not really democratic at all.

Russia, the largest of all European nations, was a thoroughgoing dictatorship under the absolute control of one man, Josef Stalin. There was a dictatorship in Turkey, under another remarkable and able man, Mustafa Kemal. Poland had started out as a democracy, but had only got into endless wrangles between the various parties; already the soldier, Marshal Pilsudski, was practically a dictator, and very soon he was to send the parliament home and become a dictator in fact. There was a weak dictatorship in Spain. Yugoslavia was finding it very difficult to settle the disputes between the two principal peoples, the Serbs and the Croats, who had combined to form the country; the government was still democratic in form, but the troubles were endless, and the shrewd King, Alexander I, was working to set up the strong dictatorial government which he afterward established. Democracy in Rumania, in Hungary, in Bulgaria, was hardly working any better. In all Central and Southeastern Europe, almost the only country in which a really democratic form of government was succeeding was Czechoslovakia, and even there the 3,500,000 German-speaking Sudetens felt that they were being oppressed by the 10,000,000 Czechs and Slovaks who had control of the government.

For those who believed that the new world must, to succeed, be a democratic world, the most serious fact was Italy. The other countries in which dictatorship had appeared were small, or unused to democratic ways. But Italy was a major power, in which parliamentary government had long existed. Yet what had happened here, after all the turmoil and upset of the war years and the first years of the peace, was not the appearance of a stronger and wiser democracy, but the rise of one man, Mussolini, who was rapidly turning the whole country into a personal absolutism. Mussolini and his Fascists declared that democracy was a worn-out idea; that parliamentary governments were silly, wasteful and inefficient; that freedom and peace were both foolish notions, and that in the future all governments would be dictatorial governments, powerfully armed in order to defend themselves against any attack or any injustice from abroad, and able to provide justice and prosperity for all at home with no nonsense about wrangling political parties and warring labor unions and the other divisions that are a part of life under a democratic state.

Some people wondered whether Mussolini might not be right, and whether all countries were not moving, some more slowly and some more rapidly, toward this kind of governance. But others said that Mussolini's dictatorship in Italy was really a kind of accident—that it happened only because Italy was comparatively a poor and backward country, and that in time Mussolini would disappear and Italy would return again to parliamentary rule. Democracy was still strong in France and Britain, the two greatest powers in Europe, and in Denmark and the Scandinavian countries, which had had enough experience with it to learn how to make it work. And more than that, Germany had gone through very much the same kind of disturbance and distress as Italy had known, and the result was not a dictatorship at all. In spite of all the troubles of the lost war and the inflation, the Communists had not seized power in Germany; neither had the reactionary Nationalists or Adolf Hitler's storm troopers. The liberal republic had come safely through all the turmoil of 1923 and 1924; it was still the government in Germany and it was one of the freest governments the world had ever known.

In Germany, from 1925 to 1930, everyone could say what he liked, think what he liked, and do very nearly anything he liked. The system of elections was an unusually democratic one. Every small party or group could send its representatives to the Reichstag, or parliament, and there make itself heard. The big liberal and democratic parties which were in control did not believe in suppression of any sort. Germans were busily experimenting with all kinds of new ideas in literature and art and architecture, and there was the greatest freedom about people's private lives. Surely, many thought, this shows the real strength of the democratic system; the dictatorships that have sprung up in so many other countries are only temporary affairs that will soon pass away.

But those who thought this way did not look closely enough at what was actually going on in Germany. The government was too free, too liberal. Countless Germans were still restless and dissatisfied under all that had happened to them since the war. The victims of the inflation did not want freedom;

they wanted the comfort and safety which they had
lost, and if they could not get that, they wanted something which would promise to get it for them. Young
men from ruined middle-class families still marched
in Hitler's storm-battalions, or listened while he
furiously denounced Jews and profiteers and the republic. The movement had lost most of its importance after the recovery from the inflation, but the
Nazi party could still claim 100,000 regular members
in 1928. Other restless young men marched with the
war veterans' organizations or voted for the extreme
reactionary Nationalist party. From the other side,
embittered workers filled the Communist ranks, to
attack the republic in their own way. And the republic, believing in freedom, did nothing against
these declared enemies. It did nothing against other
kinds of opponents. Many of its own civil servants,
and especially many of its judges, were left over from
the days of the empire, and had no real sympathy
with democracy. The army has always been a great
power in German affairs; and its conservative corps
of officers included few believers in the republican
system. But the republican governments only encouraged the army to come back to the place of power
and prestige which it had nearly lost after the great
defeat of 1918. Almost the only real believers in the
republic were the trades unionists and more conservative industrial workers of the great cities, and they
were much less than a majority of all Germans. Democracy in Germany was surrounded on all sides by

grave dangers. As long as things were going well, these were not noticeable. But once things should begin to go badly, these dangers were sure to come out in full force.

The new Europe finally put together by 1925 was not democratic, as the authors of the peace treaties had imagined that it would be. And it was not disarming. There was peace in Europe. But it was not a peace of understanding. It was a peace which was really kept by the overwhelming power of the French army, together with those of France's allies in the East—Poland and the Little Entente—and it never seemed possible to find a way in which France and her allies could be persuaded to reduce their huge military forces. But unless these big military machines could somehow be got rid of, there would be no really lasting peace or reconciliation. And there was always the chance that unless the Allies reduced their own armaments, the Germans, who bitterly resented the one-sided disarmament forced upon them by the peace treaties, would find a way of rebuilding their military strength. In these same treaties the Allies had declared their intention of reducing their own armaments as far as they could with safety, and the Germans were never tired of insisting that unless this "solemn pledge" were fulfilled, they themselves would be free to rearm. This question of armaments remained like a poison at the bottom of all the better feeling after 1925. Even Stresemann himself, at the time of the Locarno settlement, had plainly warned the world that it would have to be followed by "universal disarmament" if there was to be any real "healing from the spirit of destructiveness."

But the victor powers were making no progress whatever with the matter. As far back as 1920 the League of Nations, in one of its first acts, had set up a commission to study the problem; yet the more it was studied the more insoluble it seemed to be. The French said they could not disarm until their "security," or safety from a German attack, had been made certain. The British said that there could never be any security for anyone until the powers had disarmed. This argument was never settled. Years were spent in working out a new treaty, under which the nations would give unbreakable promises to assist each other in case one was attacked, but which would not come into force until a plan of general disarmament had been adopted. Then when the treaty was at last completed, none of the governments liked it and the whole thing was dropped.

The League tried again. It set up another commission to study the armaments themselves. This commission was not supposed to write an actual disarmament treaty, but just to prepare a kind of form for a treaty. It was to work out how, and at what points and by what rules armaments might be limited in case the powers should agree to do so; but it was to leave blank all the places where an actual treaty would have to put in definite figures—showing how many soldiers or guns or battleships each power would be allowed to keep. That would be the hard part and would have to be attended to later; but the commission's job seemed comparatively easy. Yet the commission found itself at once in endless difficulties. Its members wrangled forever over such questions as what armaments are, or how one kind of arms could be matched off against another kind. Should commercial airplanes be counted as a part of a nation's air strength, or only the military ones? Should a nation with weak industries be allowed more tanks and heavy guns than a nation with powerful industries able to make these things quickly? Should the militia and private armies, like Mussolini's Fascists or the German veteran associations and Nazi storm troopers, who did military drill, be counted as partly trained soldiers? And how many partly trained soldiers were equal to one regular soldier? And so on and so on, with the diplomats and experts of each nation always obstinately sticking to that side of the argument which would result in giving the advantage to their own country and weakening the other ones. There was no answer for such riddles, except some kind of "compromise" wording which just hid the fact that no real answer had been found; and the commission got nowhere.

And perhaps there was no answer for the one big question that really lay behind all these squabbles. That was the question of whether Europe was to continue to be controlled by a powerful French army standing over a helpless Germany, or whether Ger-

NOTE HERE !& FOOLS !

THE QUESTION OF ECONOMIC STRENGTH

many was to be brought back as an equal among other powers and Europe to be controlled by agreement among all of them. The commission wrangled on, and there was no decision one way or the other. At the time it did not seem to matter very much; people made jokes about the foolishness of the disarmament debates and the hypocrisy of the governments and paid more attention to other things. But later on they were to find out that this failure with disarmament was one of the worst failures and most dangerous weaknesses in the new Europe.

And there was one other great weakness in the new Europe, which people did not see at the time but which in the end was to do more than any other one thing to destroy the system. The nations were fairly prosperous, but the prosperity rested on a very uncertain foundation. In Germany and in most of Central Europe it was prosperity on borrowed money—borrowed from investors in France, in Great Britain and in particular in the United States. The United States in those years was going through its "boom" period that was to build up into the famous stock market speculation of 1929. Americans, or at any rate a great many Americans, were making money fast; and in the hope of making it still faster they were pouring it out into all kinds of investments and speculations not only at home but abroad as well. A great deal of this money found its way to Europe; going to work there, it helped start European factories and put Europeans back into employment and so to create more money in turn. Everyone seemed the better off for it, and as long as the Europeans could raise fresh loans to help pay back what they had already borrowed, perhaps everyone really was the better off for it. But if the rich countries should ever stop lending, an important part of European prosperity would disappear; the task of paying back the earlier loans would suddenly become very hard indeed; all the delicate adjustments of prices and wages and money values between the different countries would be thrown into confusion, and the new Europe would face a dark and difficult time.

This danger was greater because there was one particularly weak spot in the whole arrangement. The reparations problem had not really been settled. The Dawes Plan * had decided how much Germany could pay each year, but it did not say how long she would have to go on making these payments. Whatever happened, that question would have to be faced sooner or later, and until it was definitely answered there would continue to be uncertainty about the whole reparations system and its effect on the rest of European economy. But it looked as though it might not be so difficult to find an answer because of the success with which the Dawes Plan was working and the ease, and good faith, with which Germany was meeting the Dawes Plan payments.

What very few people understood at the time was the extent to which the success of the plan really depended on the loans which the German government,

* See page 52.

German towns and German industries were getting from American and other investors. There is really only one way in which a nation can pay over or "transfer" such huge sums as these to other countries. That is by sending out more actual goods or other things that people want and can use than the debtor country is bringing in. The German government, for example, could tax its own people to collect the necessary amount in marks. It would then take these marks and try to exchange them for dollars with which to pay the American government. If at the same time Germans had been selling a great deal more to Americans than they had been buying from Americans, it would mean that a lot of Americans would be trying to exchange their dollars for marks with which to pay the German exporters. The German government could then simply give its marks for the dollars of the American business men, pay the dollars to the American government, and so "transfer" its payment. But if German businesses had not been selling a "surplus" of goods to Americans, Americans would have no need of marks. The German government would find no one who wanted to give dollars for its marks; and if it tried to buy dollars anyway by offering more and more marks for each dollar, the only result would be to drive down the value of the mark until it would soon become worthless.

This was just about what had happened to bring on the terrible inflation of 1923. But after that was

↑

AND SO
GREAT
ANIMOSITY

over and the Dawes Plan was set up, Germans were
still selling no more to foreign countries than they
were buying from them. Most of the time, in fact,
they were actually buying a good deal more abroad
than they were selling there. Yet the German government paid its reparations bill regularly and without trouble. How could that happen? The answer
was in the huge sums which Germany and the Germans were borrowing from abroad. The Dawes committee saw that while Germany was still struggling
with all the wreckage of the inflation she could pay
nothing abroad with her own money; and the committee itself arranged that the other nations should
lend the German government the money to make the
first year's payments. After that, the committee
thought that Germany could find and "transfer" the
necessary amounts herself. And indeed the German
government never deliberately borrowed with one
hand what it had to pay back with the other.

What happened was that with the starting of the
Dawes Plan, German industry quickly became so
prosperous, and people in other countries became so
confident of Germany's future, that they were eager
to invest their money in any sort of German business
or lend it to any German city that asked for it. When
the German government came with its reparations
marks to exchange them into dollars or francs or
pounds, it found the dollars or francs or pounds of
these investors waiting to be changed into marks so
that they could go to work in Germany. It had no

trouble in buying foreign currencies, there was no
difficulty about "transfer." The German government
honestly raised and paid its reparations debt. But it
was able to do so only because Germany as a whole
was at the same time piling up a much bigger debt to
investors in the same countries to which reparations
payments were going. The Dawes Plan was a striking success. But what would happen if the investors
abroad ever got frightened, stopped making new
loans and demanded repayment of the old ones?

It was a question to which the statesmen and economists and bankers at the time did not pay as much
attention as they might have done. The Dawes Plan
seemed to be working so well that in barely two
years from its adoption people began to ask whether
the time had not come for fixing the full amount
which Germany would have to pay, and so at last
putting the whole reparations question away in a
permanent and definite settlement which would enable the world to forget about it. The French were
now inclined to grant further reductions in Germany's annual payments in return for such a settlement, which would take the matter out of politics
and make the debt as safe, they hoped, as any ordinary commercial debt. The Germans were inclined
to agree to a permanent settlement calling for somewhat heavier payments than they might otherwise
have accepted, because they wanted France to take
her troops out of the Rhineland, which France was
occupying under the terms of the Versailles treaty

until Germany should prove that she was willing and able to live up to her reparations obligations.

In September, 1926, Briand and Stresemann, the two foreign ministers, met for the friendliest of luncheons in the garden of a simple inn in the little village of Thoiry, near Geneva. The Frenchman, with his straggling hair, his long, droopy mustaches and an untidy cigarette usually hanging from the corner of his mouth, and the big, fat, bullet-headed German, were very different-looking people, but they always got on well together. They talked over the whole reparations business; and then, it is said, had a friendly argument afterward over who should pay for the luncheon, which Briand ended by snatching up the check and saying: "Let me do this; you still have to pay reparations!" Nothing came of the meeting at that time, but negotiations went on, and two years later it was decided to set up a new committee to go over the Dawes Plan and prepare a final settlement. Again it was a committee of experts, not of political representatives, and again an American, Owen D. Young, was made its head. But this time German representatives had a place upon the committee along with the victor powers; the new settlement, instead of being dictated to Germany by the others, was to be the result of free negotiation. The Young committee worked all through the first part of 1929, and the governments held an international conference later in the year to study its report and arrange all the practical details of the new plan which

it recommended. There were many bitter disputes between Germany and the creditor powers, and between the creditor powers themselves, over the division of the payments, but in the end every difficulty was overcome. In January, 1930, the Young Plan, as it is called, was at last adopted.

Germany promised to pay roughly from $400,-000,000 to $600,000,000 a year over the next fifty-nine years. The Allies agreed among themselves as to how they would share the payments; many complicated details were adjusted, and it was provided that when this great scheme had finally been worked out to its end in the year 1988, Germany would be held to have met fully and completely every claim for reparations under the Versailles treaty. The Young Plan was a truly remarkable triumph of negotiation, compromise and adjustment. M. Briand saw even greater hopes, and in these same months began to talk about a plan—he never made it very precise or definite—for a "United States of Europe" in which all the powers that had fought each other so fiercely in the World War would settle their differences and work together for the good of the Continent.

But it happened that in October, 1929, Stresemann, who had so often worked with Briand and who was one of the few statesmen in Europe who could have helped such dreams to come true, died suddenly at the early age of fifty-one. And a week or two later there was a change of government in France; Briand went out of office and a more conservative Premier, who was much more bitter toward Germany and less inclined to make peace with her, took office. Such changes might not have greatly mattered in the long run. But it was also in October, 1929, that there came the famous crash on the New York Stock Exchange. It meant that the American "boom" was over. It meant that the hundreds of millions of dollars which had been pouring into foreign lending simply dried up and vanished. It meant that the Great Depression, following, after eleven years, in the wake of the Great War, had begun. The Young Plan was supposed to last until 1988. Actually, before it had even been finally adopted, the conditions on which it rested had all been changed. Prosperity was about to go. The loans from America and from the other countries were soon to stop. The feeling of friendliness and conciliation was soon to dwindle away, as the governments found themselves struggling with greater and greater difficulties and the people of each nation tried to blame their troubles on the others. Although it was to take a little time for people to realize it, the bottom had been knocked out of the new Europe which had been set up in 1925; and in the general collapse all the hidden weaknesses and dangers in the system were quickly to appear.

Some people like to ask whether, if the Great Depression had not come as it did, the new Europe might not have slowly overcome those weaknesses, got rid of the dangers, and developed into a peaceful and prosperous community. It is probably a useless question, because the depression really grew out of the kind of world which had been put together after the Great War. To have had no depression, it would have been necessary to have put together a different kind of world. Yet there was a great deal of hope in the years from 1925 to 1930, and many good beginnings out of which it is hard not to believe that something better than still another great war might have come. However that may be, with the coming of the depression the whole scene changed.

4. THE KEYSTONE CRACKS

ALL OVER THE WORLD PROSPERITY had begun to dribble away even before the Wall Street crash showed people what was happening; in many parts of Europe the pressure of loss, of poverty and dissatisfaction was rising, and through the first months of 1930 it was to rise very fast indeed. But it was in one of the smallest of the European countries that the effects were first felt most severely and with, as it turned out, the worst results for the whole post-war system.

Little Austria was a kind of keystone in the arch which had finally been put together. You can see it by looking at the map. She separated Germany from Italy. She separated Germany from Hungary and from Yugoslavia. She protected the southern side of Czechoslovakia, which was the almost open back door into the natural fortress formed by the chains of mountains within which that country lay. With a strong and independent Austria, all these countries would feel fairly safe from Germany and could more easily work out their own problems with each other. The French would feel much safer because of the safety of their allies in the Little Entente, and because they need not fear that the 6,500,000 German-speaking Austrians would be added to the man-power of Germany, which was already greater than that of France. If Austria should collapse, everything would be upset; every power would have to make different arrangements for its defense, and the feeling of comparative security and good will behind the "Locarno spirit" would disappear at once. The peace treaties had forever forbidden the union of Austria with Germany—the *Anschluss* as it was called—and the existence of an independent Austria, strong and united and able to look out for herself, as was Switzerland, was necessary to the success of the settlement which rested on the Locarno agreements.

But Austria was neither strong, nor united, nor in-

dependent. Although she was the keystone, she was
also one of the weakest stones in the European arch.
The peace treaties had commanded that she forever
stand alone, but they had given her no means of doing
so, and it was only through loans and help from
abroad that the country had been propped up and
kept alive at all. Many Austrians did not want independence. They believed that only by *Anschluss* with
Germany could the country find an economic base
broad enough to survive on. The country was not
united. It was torn by a violent hostility between the
working masses of Vienna, who were liberal and
Socialist in their politics, and the country people, who
were conservative and devoutly Catholic. Two rival
private armies grew up—the Heimwehr, or home
guard, of the conservatives, and the Schutzbund, or
defense corps, of the Viennese workers—both ille-
gally armed. The city government of Vienna was
firmly in the hands of the Social Democrats; the government of the country was through many years
conducted by Monsignor Seipel, a shrewd and thin-
lipped Catholic prelate and politician, who had behind him a coalition of the conservative and reactionary parties just strong enough to outvote the Socialists. His policy in general was to strengthen the reactionary and anti-republican Heimwehr and to
break the power of the trades unions and Socialists
in what the conservatives called "Red Vienna." But,
as in so many other countries, neither side was quite

strong enough to destroy the other, and really govern.

There had been one terrible day in Vienna, far back in the summer of 1927, when a vast workers' demonstration had met the police; the police were foolish and the marchers lost their heads, and a bloody battle raged for hours through the center of the capital. The police fired wildly into the dense crowds; the crowds tore up bricks and paving stones, robbed a gun shop, broke into and burned down the Palace of Justice and blocked the arriving fire engines, until their own Socialist Mayor of Vienna jumped on a fire-ladder and shouted to them to be sensible. Eighty-five of the people and four police officers were killed on that long, wild day. The rioting finally died down; but the memory did not. The workers nicknamed Chancellor Seipel the "No-Mercy Cardinal"; the Chancellor set himself more firmly than ever against any idea of co-operation with the masses of "Red Vienna," while the Heimwehr grew and the hostility on both sides deepened. Austria was anything but united, and that meant that she was anything but strong.

On this shaky state the depression fell with a disastrous impact. As the year 1930 wore on, the government found its expenses rising and its revenues falling. It could not raise more in taxes; it could not effect economies; it could not even get a majority at the polls. There was an election in October; the conservative government coalition was beaten, but it remained in office anyway, relying on the power of the Heimwehr gangs, who were denouncing democratic government and calling for dictatorship. It was, as it turned out, the last election ever held under the Austrian Republic. In Austria's great neighbor, Germany, at the same time, a moderate Catholic Chancellor, Bruening, was struggling with the same kind of difficulties. He had no firm parliamentary majority behind him in the Reichstag; with expenses rising and income drying up, he could not get his budget bill adopted; while Adolf Hitler's storm troopers were now going up and down the country organizing meetings, riots, and street fights.

There was a clause in the German constitution under which in an emergency the President could authorize the Chancellor to disregard the Reichstag and govern by simple decree. In order to get his budget enacted, Chancellor Bruening took up this dangerous weapon; free government was suspended and the budget put through. But the republic in Germany was never really to recover. That September a new Reichstag election was held. All through August Hitler and his Nazis had flung themselves with the utmost fury into the electoral campaign. With many of the big conservative industrialists behind him because they thought him a useful safeguard against Communism, Hitler had plenty of money. His brownshirts stormed and rioted through the streets, tearing down Communist posters and breaking up Communist meetings and parades; while "the Leader" himself was racing by airplane and motorcar from one monster assembly to another, stirring them to frenzies of enthusiasm with his pageantry and his oratory, and the lesser Nazi chiefs were shrieking their promises and denunciations to smaller gatherings held by the thousand all over Germany. But few, even of the Germans, were prepared for the result. When the ballots were counted the Nazi party had 6,406,000 votes—about one-fifth of the whole—and 107 seats in the Reichstag. At one jump it had become the second-largest party in Germany.

The rest of the world was astounded—and alarmed. It had thought of Hitler as just a wild and ignorant agitator, of no importance in himself and with a fantastically impossible program. But here he was suddenly the leader of the second-largest German party, with a powerful private army behind him; and he was shouting for the end of reparations, for the tearing up of the Versailles treaty, for the rearmament of Germany, for dictatorship and for war if necessary. He was as wild as ever. He was preaching a base and reckless anti-Semitism and his followers were smashing Jewish shop windows and insulting Jews on the streets. A few days after the election he was publicly declaring that the Nazis would soon control Germany and that when they did people would see his opponents' heads "rolling in the sand." But this was a wild man who was now promising to destroy the whole foundation on which the new Europe rested—and who might soon have the power to do so. A wave of nervous anger went through France and her eastern allies; everywhere other peoples began to think about their own armaments; everywhere the old bitterness against Germany and the fear of German aggression began to revive.

But Bruening managed to get a shaky majority in the new Reichstag in spite of the Nazis, and continued, as did the Austrian government, in the hopeless fight against the depression. He appealed to the other powers. Unless the reparations payments could be ended, he argued, Germany would be bankrupt again; but the creditor nations were suspicious and thought he was exaggerating. Then in March, 1931, a new idea was tried. Suddenly the German and Austrian governments announced a plan for a customs union between the two countries—a plan, that is, under which the governments of the two countries would remain separate as before, but their tariff and economic systems would become one. It would probably have done a good deal to help both nations out of their economic difficulties. But the French, already alarmed by Hitler's successes, were horrified at this. In effect it meant, they said, the *Anschluss*, forever forbidden by the Versailles treaty; it meant the end of the treaties; it meant that there would be 6,500,000 more people to feed the German armies; it meant the end of security for France. The French tried in every way to block the plan; and one way in which they are supposed to have acted was to draw their money out of German and Austrian banks, thus further weakening an already tottering economic structure.

It was in little Austria that the first great crash of the new European system began. In May the huge Credit Anstalt bank in Vienna suddenly collapsed, and a wave of economic crises spread out through Europe and the world. Outside loans were desperately needed if the whole Austrian financial system was not to go down, but the French refused to help unless the customs union plan was definitely abandoned; and while the statesmen and financiers wrangled, the damage rapidly widened. By June the German banks were tottering; Bruening and his Finance Minister were rushing from one European capital to another begging help, while behind them money was draining rapidly out of Germany and important firms were beginning to fail. On June 18 Hindenburg, the old general who had been commander-in-chief of the German armies during the war and had since become President of the German Republic, appealed directly to President Hoover in Washington: "Relief must come at once." Mr. Hoover, who was already seriously disturbed, sat down to work the long-distance telephone, consulting the principal Congressional and financial leaders; and on Saturday evening, June 20, he suddenly announced to the world his proposal that all reparations payments by Germany and war debt payments by the Allies to the United States should cease for a year. It was the famous "Hoover moratorium."

But to arrange the details took time. The French hesitated to break so big a hole through the financial clauses of the Versailles treaty, and they could not be brought to agree until July 6. A few days later one of the largest banks in Germany failed and every other bank in the country had to be closed. In time, and with the help of the moratorium, the other powers were able to patch things up and get Germany and Austria going again. But the financial crisis could not be stopped. The effects spread to London; and in September the world was shocked to hear that Great Britain, which men had thought of for generations as the strong and stable money capital of the earth, had been forced to abandon the gold standard. All around the world the "economic blizzard" raged; the depression deepened; the governments were left floundering in more difficulties than ever and the peoples were sunk further than before in loss, in fear and in hostility toward each other. And another thing had happened. The moratorium on the reparations and debt payments was supposed to last a year. It will probably last forever. Germany has never paid another cent of reparations, nor have the Allies on their war debts.

The peace treaties included three main sections—the political or territorial settlements, the military or disarmament settlements and the financial or reparations settlements. These were the three foundation pillars of the new Europe. One of these three great pillars had now fallen, beyond hope of rebuilding.

How long could the others last? Three days before Great Britain left the gold standard, a strange affair took place on the opposite side of the world— at Mukden in Manchuria, which was then still a part of China. A bomb went off on the tracks of the Japanese-owned railway. It was at night; who planted the bomb or why has never been definitely learned, but before morning the Japanese soldiery were storming through Mukden, disarming the Chinese troops and driving them from the city, while their spokesmen declared that the Chinese had set the bomb and that Japan, in order to protect her great interests in Manchuria, would have to take control of the country. The long war of Japanese conquest in China—a war which has gone on, with some intervals, ever since and has spread from Manchuria far into the heart of the vast Chinese territory —had begun.

To most of the rest of the world it seemed an outrageous act of violent aggression, like Mussolini's sudden bombardment of Corfu, years before; and as the Greeks had done then, the Chinese protested vigorously to the League of Nations. But, though this was a much more serious case than that of Corfu, the League in the end was to do even less about it. It made motions. It held meetings; it sent a commission into Manchuria which studied the matter and wrote a report condemning Japan as an aggressor. Japan merely announced that she would resign from the League; her army went on to seize all of Manchuria, while far away to the southward her navy began a terrible attack upon the Chinese part of Shanghai—a bloody small war in itself, in which thousands of Chinese civilians as well as soldiers died and great sections of the city were destroyed in flames and artillery fire. And the League—its member powers divided, uncertain and suspicious of each other—did nothing. Many said that it did not really matter, because after all Manchuria was far away on the other side of the world and of small concern to the great European nations. But some others wondered whether this did not already prove the feebleness and uselessness of the League of Nations, and whether another time of violence and aggressive war was not beginning.

If so, how long could disarmament—which had never got farther than the disarming of Germany, Austria and Hungary—last? In February, 1932, a formal Disarmament Conference finally met at Geneva, after twelve years of wrangling "preparation." It met with the tramp of the Japanese armies in Manchuria and the blast of the Japanese bombs at Shanghai in every delegate's mind. It met; it argued; it proposed plans, and it accomplished nothing. As before, every plan proposed was really only a plan for weakening other nations' armaments and making the nation proposing it stronger by comparison. And all the plans broke up against what had always been the one great question. Was European peace to be maintained by keeping Germany weak and France and Britain powerful? Or was it to be maintained by inviting Germany to come back as a great power, as strongly armed as any other and therefore willing to be peaceful?

It was the old question; but now it was faced in a new situation. In Germany, Adolf Hitler and his brown-shirt army seemed to be growing in power every day. Chancellor Bruening, the Social Democrats, all parties which believed in the republic, seemed to be growing weaker. The French, the British and the Americans (who were also members of the conference) could see that unless they yielded something to Bruening and the republican government, it would only lose ground the faster to Hitler's ferocious nationalism; at the same time, with every fresh success of the Nazi storm battalions, the French and British were only more afraid that if they yielded anything Germany would take everything, while any arms granted to Bruening and the republic might soon be wielded by the aggressive spirit of Hitlerism.

In March and April, 1932, presidential elections were held in Germany. Hindenburg, the old general, was re-elected with 53 per cent of the final vote; but Adolf Hitler, who ran against him in another whirl-wind Nazi campaign, received 36.8 per cent. Amid the fierce and savage nationalism of the Nazis, the timidity of the Social Democrats, the weakness of the moderate, middle-of-the-road parties like the Catholic "Centrum" to which Bruening belonged, and the readiness of the nobles, the conservative industrial magnates and the monarchists to support the Nazis in order to destroy Communism and liberalism, it was rapidly becoming impossible for republican government to work in Germany. No one had a real majority. The Nazis were gaining every day, partly because of the depression, partly because of their lavish promises, partly because they were organized to fight for success with propaganda, rioting and intimidation. The only way to stop them was to fight back. But the Social Democrats, the great party of the German trades unions and workers, did not believe in fighting back by such means. In May Bruening was forced out of the Chancellorship. He was succeeded by a queer figure—Franz von Papen, an aristocrat, a conservative, a former diplomat and an intriguer who had set out to use the Nazis in order to smash the Communist and liberal forces in the republic and to place himself and his rich and noble friends in control of Germany.

On the last day of July there was another Reichstag election. Hitler and his Nazis still failed of a majority. But they won 37 per cent of the voters and 230 seats; with almost twice as many votes as the Social Democrats they had become, in another great leap, by far the largest German party. The confusion was bad enough already; matters rapidly became impossible. The Nazi riots, shootings and bombings reached a new peak. The old President called Hitler in and offered him a position in the government; he refused, unless he were made Chancellor and placed at its head. Hindenburg would not give him that power while the disorders of his brown-shirt followers continued. Von Papen tried to carry on the government, but only under greater and greater difficulties. Every sort of combination of parties, with the Nazis or without the Nazis, was attempted in the effort to get a firm governmental majority. None succeeded. A new election was called for November.

Surprisingly enough, the Nazis noticeably lost ground. They received only 32 per cent instead of 37 per cent of the vote; their Reichstag seats dropped from 230 to 196. The Nazi leaders were frightened, and the party itself was beginning to show signs of going to pieces between its own radical and conservative wings. Hindenburg was still refusing to make Hitler Chancellor because he believed the result would be a Nazi dictatorship and the end of the republic, which the "old gentleman" was pledged to preserve. But if the Nazis were weakening, they had already brought German politics and government to an incurable confusion. Von Papen was still unable to put together a working government, and was replaced by an army general, Schleicher, who made his own attempts to combine the warring parties into some kind of basis for a government. The most he accomplished was to win a breathing-space of a few weeks. Nothing was really settled. But as the year ran out, the Disarmament Conference at Geneva at last agreed on a "formula" under which the Allies

and the United States recognized Germany's theo-
retical right to have armaments equal to their own.
It was a victory of a kind for the German Republic.
But it was not much, and it came far too late.

For the German Republic was dying—just as the
Italian parliamentary democracy had died years before, but more swiftly, more suddenly, with a greater
violence. As the new year, 1933, came in the depression was everywhere at its worst. In Germany, von
Papen was intriguing against Schleicher, was confer-
ring with the Nazis and was working on the old
President to overcome his reluctance to bring Hitler
into power. Millions of Germans, non-Nazis as well
as Nazis, were coming to believe that the confusion
was hopeless, that the republic could never be made
to work again, that something else would have to be
tried if Germany were not simply to fall to pieces
in revolution and civil war. Von Papen had a great
scheme. Hitler should be made Chancellor, but with
von Papen as Vice-Chancellor and with a cabinet
containing a majority of conservatives and only a
minority of Nazi representatives. In this way the
wealthy and conservative elements would use Hitler's vast popular following, his parades and propaganda and storm troopers, to establish themselves in
power. Afterward, they would be able to check
Hitler's wild policies, tame his Nazi movement, and
set up an orderly, conservative control of the country. Von Papen and his associates finally won over
the aged Hindenburg, who had promised to defend

the republic. On January 30, 1933, Adolf Hitler, the war-time corporal who had joined a six-man "party" in a Munich beer-hall fourteen years before, became Chancellor of Germany.

It was the end of republican government in Germany. It was the end, though few people knew it at the time, of a vast number of other things in the Europe which had been put together after the conclusion of the World War. The collapse of that new Europe had already begun. From this moment onward it was to proceed swiftly and disastrously.

PART TWO

THE COLLAPSE OF EUROPE

5. THE "YEAR OF BLOOD": 1934

VON PAPEN HAD BROUGHT HITLER
into power as the tool of himself and his clever, conservative friends. Within little more than a month
Hitler and his Nazis had made themselves the masters
of Germany; within little more than a year nearly
every trace of republican Germany had been wiped
out, and the Nazi dictatorship, absolutely in the
hands of this one strange, shrewd, moody and fanatic
man, had established itself in unshakable control
over every smallest side of German life. As Hitler
took office he issued a proclamation. After thirteen
years, it declared, his party had come to power; "the
struggle to win the German people, however, is only
beginning." A new election was ordered, and the
Nazis launched another furious electoral campaign,
of the familiar kind.

But this time there was a difference. The government and the police were now largely in Nazi hands.
The Communists were forbidden to hold meetings
and the homes of their leaders were raided. The
police were ordered to shoot "Communist terrorists"

on sight. Socialist newspapers were suppressed. All newspaper criticism of Hitler was forbidden. There were huge Nazi meetings, vast public demonstrations, all the old oratory with its vague but exciting promises of a new Germany, a strong and united Germany that would break the "shackles" of the peace treaties, destroy radicals and Marxists, punish "Jewish traitors" and bring prosperity to everyone. In spite of everything, however, the Nazis were not sure. Their vote had fallen off last time. Some of those who had helped them to office were already regretting what they had done. Many Germans, perhaps, were getting tired of violence and terrorism in the streets and the endless Nazi parades.

The election was to be on March 5, 1933. On the evening of February 27 a young man walking home past the huge (and ugly) bulk of the Reichstag building in Berlin glanced up and saw someone on a balcony near the main door with what seemed to be a torch in his hand. The passer-by ran for a policeman. Other strollers saw the same figure on the balcony, and what looked like fire in a ground-floor room, and also summoned the police. The latter seem to have been a little slow in moving; but at any rate, by the time the alarm was fully given and fire-engines began to arrive, the great central chamber where the Reichstag held its sessions was blazing furiously, and the fire beyond control. The flames were still roaring through the structure when the high Nazi chiefs, Goering and Goebbels, arrived

upon the scene. By that time the police had found
and dragged out of the building a half-witted Dutch
boy, with some connection with the Communist
party, who had apparently been helping set the fire.
Goering said afterward that he knew at once that
this was a Communist plot; and before midnight
orders had gone out for the arrest of every Communist leader whom the police could lay their hands on.

Who was actually responsible for the burning of
the Reichstag building is not known, but there seems
plenty of reason for supposing that it was the Nazis
themselves. At any rate, the whole Nazi propaganda
machinery seized upon the affair at once. The story
was spread up and down Germany, in every exciting
and dramatic way possible, that the Communists had
fired the Reichstag as a signal for a Communist revolution throughout Germany—a revolution which had
only been prevented by the promptness with which
the Nazis had acted. In the three or four days remaining before the election fear and excitement were
worked up to their highest pitch, while new terror
and suppressions beat down all opposition to the
Nazis. The vote was held. The Nazis still received
only 44 per cent of the ballots and considerably less
than a majority of the Reichstag seats. But it was
enough. The Nazis were as strong as the three next-
strongest parties combined; Hitler now had the
power to do what he wanted, and step by step he
went on to do it, while the outside world watched
with shocked astonishment.

He demanded from the Reichstag the right to rule by decree; it was granted him, and he then sent the Reichstag home. It was the end of parliamentary government in Germany. One by one the conservatives were maneuvered out of the Cabinet, their places being taken by Nazi chieftains. The rights of free speech and a free press were rapidly suppressed and the newspapers and publishing houses were brought into Nazi hands. The trades unions were destroyed and replaced by Nazi unions, which were little more than devices through which the party could compel the workers to obey its orders. A cruel persecution of the Jews began; it was to go on, growing worse year by year, as the Nazis used the Jews as scapegoats for every misfortune of the past and as victims sacrificed to keep up the enthusiasm of the party followers. The concentration camps—great prisons into which men were thrust without trial, without even formal arrest, often without notice to their families—were established and filled with Jews, with Communists, with liberals and anyone else who dared oppose the Hitler government. The schools were brought under strict control; the textbooks were rewritten and strange doctrines about the importance of race, the superiority of the German race above all others, the necessity for being strong in war and the "weakness" of such Christian virtues as forgiveness and sacrifice and pacifism—doctrines which seemed fantastically untrue and wicked to others—were drilled into German children as well as grown-ups.

The Nazi dictatorship seemed somewhat more extravagant, more violent, more cruel and more backward in its ideas than the other dictatorships which had appeared; but those were not the reasons why it shook the whole European system. After all, the great Western democratic powers had watched much the same kind of thing going on in Russia and Italy and the smaller countries without being greatly worried by it. But here was a dictatorship which not only destroyed freedom and democratic government at home; its leaders declared over and over again that they would destroy every important element of the 1919 peace settlements, which were all that were holding Europe together. Nearly every misfortune of Germany they blamed on what they called the "dictate" of Versailles. If there was poverty in Germany, it was because of the reparations payments and because of the loss of those territories of which Germany had been "robbed" by the peace treaties. German "rights" were being trampled on and Germany was being kept weak and helpless by the Allied powers with their great armies and navies; Germany must have armaments of her own as strong as those of the nations surrounding her.

The Nazis denied that Germany had been beaten in 1918. They rewrote their history books to prove that what really happened was that the German armies in the field were "stabbed in the back" by the revolution, inspired by Jews and Communists, which broke out at home. Everything that followed must be undone. Germany would never again make reparations payments. She must have back her colonies that had been taken from her in 1918. She must have back her lost European territories, such as the Polish "Corridor" which divided East Prussia from the rest of Germany. If the other powers were really peaceful and just, they would give her these things. But Germany must be strong enough to demand them. She must be ready to fight for what she needed; the one thing that made a people great and happy was victory in war, and the one highest duty of every German citizen was to give his life, if necessary, on the battlefield.

Here was a dictatorship, in other words, determined to upset the economic arrangements, the territorial settlements and the military balance which had been set up in 1919, and according to which all the European nations were living and adjusting their policies. It was a dictatorship which despised the League of Nations, which jeered at the idea of peace, which from the moment it came to power had begun secretly arming itself—and which governed with an iron hand the second-largest European people. No one had felt too safe or certain before; there were few who could feel either now. But no one knew just what to do about it or could agree on doing anything.

In France, in Great Britain and in many of the smaller countries there were those who feared and hated the Nazis, who saw them as a great peril which

would surely break out upon the rest of Europe unless the other powers were ready to check them by
force. But there were many others who could never
quite bring themselves to believe that Hitler and his

CENTRAL EUROPE: 1920

associates really meant what they said, who were sure
that the responsibility of governing would tame all
this wild barbarism and who shrank from the risks of
war and the costs of heavy rearmament which a
policy of suppression would involve. After all, these
people said, there was a great deal of justice in many
of the German demands; the sensible thing to do was

to yield to Hitler what he could in fairness ask and so come to a friendly agreement with him. There were still others who were much more afraid of the spread of Communism in their own countries under the strains of the depression than they were of Hitler's warlike talk; they rather admired the way in which the Nazis had smashed radicalism of all kinds in Germany; and they were anxious that Hitler should not be overthrown because they thought the result would be a Communist revolution which would first sweep Germany and then, perhaps, the rest of the world.

These people, many of them among the rich and powerful, were slow to give any encouragement to the idea of taking warlike measures against the Nazis in defense of the post-war system. And there were still others—very few of them in England, rather more in France—who were feeling the same disgust with democratic government that the Germans had felt; who liked the idea of marching together in storm battalions, of saluting a strong leader, of sweeping all confusions away to become part of a great, disciplined, unified and warlike nation. Sir Oswald Mosley's blackshirts in England, and the veteran and monarchist and patriotic societies in France sprang up to imitate the Nazis, to browbeat and battle with radicals in the streets and to spread the idea of dictatorship in their own countries.

The coming to power of the Nazis in Germany

threatened everything that was fixed and stable in post-war Europe. But among all these different ideas the other great nations could come to no firm policy. They could neither make room for the new Nazi Germany nor resolve to put her down by force while there was still time. The diplomats and statesmen hurried here and there, trying many ideas and accomplishing very little. In the summer of 1933 there was a great World Economic Conference in London which was supposed to deal seriously with the common problems of the depression, but which accomplished nothing. Then in October disarmament received its final blow. The Disarmament Conference had been dragging along; the Germans had been promised equality in principle, but no one had ever discovered how to give it to them in fact. Suddenly Hitler ordered his representatives to leave Geneva and announced that Germany would withdraw from the League of Nations. Everybody knew what it meant. Everyone knew that Germany would rearm of her own accord; but no one knew what to do about it. It was the first of Hitler's many sudden movements, so abrupt as to catch the other powers off their guard, not quite serious enough for any of them to threaten a war to prevent it, but at the same time paving the way for another step that would be more serious still. It succeeded perfectly. The Disarmament Conference had been broken up and nothing happened.

Meanwhile, the various powers had been trying,

in their different ways, new diplomatic combinations that would protect them. In France there was now a "Left" or liberal government again; and French statesmen began to think in a more friendly way of Soviet Russia. They remembered the old pre-war alliance between France and Russia; they knew that for years Hitler and his Nazis had been denouncing the Bolshevists as the worst criminals in Europe and the Continent's greatest danger; and the French began to wonder whether they might not be able to make something like another alliance with Russia to help in keeping down this new Germany that threatened to become so powerful. Mussolini, who had denounced Bolshevism almost as vigorously as the Germans, had a different idea. He suggested a four-power alliance of England, France, Germany and Italy to keep peace in Europe. This would have meant a much stronger and more influential position for Italy. But it would also have meant the end of the League of Nations as an effective body. The French and British, who dominated the League, had no desire to invite Germany and Italy to a position of equal power with themselves; while the smaller nations, who found that the League gave them their only chance of making themselves heard at all, objected violently.

The smaller powers had their own ideas. The nations of the Little Entente—Czechoslovakia, Rumania and Yugoslavia—tightened up their understanding and agreed to conduct their foreign and economic policies together. Poland began to abandon her old association with France; she tried to keep herself free from any alliances and make friends both with Russia on one side of her and with Germany on the other. Greece and Turkey began to forget their old disputes and work for an agreement with Yugoslavia and Rumania that would protect the Balkan region. But none of all this could really mean very much if a great crisis came. The diplomats hurried about; but so did armament salesmen, so did the propagandists, shrieking their hatreds and insults, so did politicians and agitators within the different countries, talking in ever more violent terms and seeming to be constantly more bitter, more unreasonable and more reckless. Within the nations as well as between them, a sort of savage gangsterism seemed to be creeping across Europe; and men who tried to look ahead could see nothing except a greater confusion, a greater tendency to extremes and an ever greater threat of war.

Nineteen-thirty-four was a strange and violent year. Its troubles began on a raw February afternoon in Paris, when enormous crowds poured suddenly out on the boulevards, and stones began to whistle past the heads of the police in the packed Place de la Concorde, the great square beside the River Seine. It was the climax of the long trail of political scandals arising out of the Stavisky affair. Caught in a large-scale swindle, this shady financial manipulator had committed suicide some weeks before; it had then begun to appear that the police authorities were implicated in his operations and, above them, many prominent figures in the Left government itself. These evidences of corruption in high places had caused a tremendous excitement and had come as a severe shock to public confidence at a particularly bad time. Everywhere people were feeling disgusted with the government, tired of the politicians, tired and doubtful, even, of the democratic system itself. As had happened in Italy and Germany and other countries, people were beginning to feel that there must be a change, that they wanted something different, but did not know what. The newspapers and politicians of the Right seized upon the Stavisky scandals as ammunition for furious attacks on the Left parties which were in power; but in addition the war veterans' associations and reactionary patriotic leagues—imitators of the early Fascist and Nazi organizations—were exploiting the excitement in what seemed to be an attempt to abolish parliamentary government altogether.

In their gray building across the river from the Place de la Concorde, the Chamber of Deputies (the lower house of the French parliament) had met that day. "Nobody who did not see it could believe the passion and hate which was shown between the Right and the Left" as the torrents of oratory poured forth. Outside the building, at the same time, the patriotic leagues and the war veterans' societies were organizing street demonstrations and parades which

were to converge upon the Chamber; the Communists were gathering for answering demonstrations,
while hundreds of thousands of restless spectators
swelled the crowds. The largest numbers collected
in the Place de la Concorde, and rioting began there
soon after five o'clock. There were many minor
scuffles; paving stones and iron gratings were
wrenched loose to be used as weapons; automobiles
were overturned and barricades thrown up in the
side streets, and at about eight in the evening a mass
movement began toward the bridge leading over the
river to the Chamber of Deputies. A French flag was
advancing across the square as a rallying-point; the
mobs were singing the "Marseillaise," shouting, "On
to the Chamber!" "Down with Parliament!" "Resign, Resign!" At the bridge, fire hoses were turned
upon the leading masses, but they could not stop by
that time even if they had wanted to as the crowds
behind pushed them on. The police had already been
forced halfway back across the bridge when shooting began. The bridge was held. But as the crowds
fell back leaving dead and wounded on the pavement
they were in a ferocious temper. "Assassins!" All
that night, all next day and evening, rioting went on
through the Paris streets. Official figures listed a
dozen killed, five or six hundred in hospital and a
thousand more treated in first-aid stations and sent
home; but observers believed that the actual casual-
ties had been far greater.

Was democracy in France about to come to the

same violent end which it had met in Italy and Germany? It did not, of course. A new government was formed, order was restored and the French Republic showed itself much more durable than younger democracies. But no one could know this at the time, and many were still anxiously watching these events in France, when there came another shocking explosion from a little farther to the east. It was early on the morning of February 8 that the police finally cleared the last mobs from the Paris boulevards. In Vienna on that same day the Austrian authorities announced that they had discovered "an unprecedented criminal plot of Bolshevist and Marxist elements." In a series of raids the police had discovered hidden stores of rifles and machineguns which had been laid away by the republican Schutzbund—the workers' private army—when it had been declared illegal. Schutzbund leaders were arrested; the offices of a leading Socialist newspaper were seized. Many had their doubts as to whether there was really a revolutionary plot, but it was easy to see in this announcement the sign of a coming storm.

Austria, the weak keystone in the arch of Europe, had been further cracking under new dangers and difficulties. The quarrel between the Socialist workers of Vienna and the conservative and Catholic parties had been complicated by a new menace. Hitler and his Nazis had come to power in Germany; one of their chief demands was the union of Austria with Germany, and they had set out to achieve it by encouraging an Austrian Nazi party. Supported by German money and leadership, the Austrian Nazis were filling the little country with violent riotings and outrages. So Austria was now torn among three main groups, each bitterly hostile to the others, and unless something was done they would end by tearing her to pieces. But what was to be done?

The head of the government was now Engelbert Dollfuss, a conservative, a devout Catholic and a follower of Monsignor Seipel, the "No-Mercy Cardinal" who had guided the country for so long. Dollfuss was a little, almost a tiny man—the jokers called him the "Vest-Pocket Chancellor"—but he had a great courage in his small body. What he did not have, perhaps, was enough wisdom; maybe few men, however, could have been wise enough to meet the problem before him. He could have made peace with the Vienna workers and asked them to help him put down the Nazis; but the workers were distrustful. His own followers hated and feared the "Reds" and "Marxists," and were not anxious to deal too severely with the Nazis, whom they thought of as a protection against radicalism. He could have made peace with the Nazis, and used them to help in doing away with the republic, stamping out Socialism and breaking the power of the workers' organizations. But that would mean only that the Nazis would in turn smash his own government and hand Austria over to the Hitler dictatorship. What Dollfuss tried to do was fight both the Nazis and the Socialist workers at the same time.

The wild happenings in France had helped to fill Austria with excitement and high tension; the police raids showed that something was coming, and on February 12 it came. The day before there had been a raid on the Socialist headquarters in the town of Linz; the Socialists had resisted and there had been a small battle. By the morning, the news was all over Vienna. This, people said, meant civil war; it meant that there must be a general strike, that the Socialists must fight back. It was a cold, gray winter morning; about eleven o'clock the lights suddenly went out and the street cars stopped running. Someone had pulled the switches at the power stations. Nobody on either side seemed to know whether this was the beginning of a general strike or not, but the government and the Heimwehr—the conservative private army which now held a position of great power with the government—prepared to hit and to hit hard. The streets were suddenly filled with police, with troops and with armed Heimwehr detachments; there was a declaration of martial law, and then, in the course of the afternoon, there came from one of the workers' districts the terrible sound of rifle and machinegun fire. The police had been raiding a huge workers' tenement house when a shot had been fired —no one knows from which side—and the battle had begun. The troops stormed through the building, clearing out the men, women and children in it.

The great pride of the Socialist city government of Vienna was the fine, modern workers' houses which it had built during the previous years. These were big blocks of buildings, constructed around large central courtyards—an arrangement intended to give sun and play space and safety from traffic to those who lived in them, but an arrangement which now made them into something very much like fortresses. In them, too, the workers of the Socialist Schutzbund had buried or bricked up their arms and ammunition, when the Schutzbund had been declared illegal. As the troops and the Heimwehr now advanced upon these buildings, the people living in them resolved to defend their homes.

Many of the Schutzbund leaders had been arrested in the previous raids; without them, the Schutzbund was disorganized; often there were none beside these leaders who knew just where the arms were concealed. But men and women set themselves frantically to digging away the courtyards or tearing down brickwork in a search for the weapons; many were found; gateways and windows were manned, barricades were thrown up and trench systems dug here and there through fields between the buildings. As evening came on a real civil war was raging in half a dozen places; there was a great deal of machinegun fire rattling through the city, and then, after dark, people all over Vienna suddenly heard the heavier boom and thud of artillery. The troops were shelling the model houses of the workers.

"All that night the sound of machineguns and the rifle fire never ceased in Vienna . . . and the sun had hardly risen before the artillery was again firing." In places children lay flat on the floor of their own apartments while the rifle bullets whined past their heads through the shattered windows just above them. The fighting had begun on a Monday; all Tuesday and Wednesday it went on, the big dwelling houses being smashed by shellfire, or taken by storm, one after the other, and the thousands who lived in them turned bodily into the chilly streets. It was a savage and shocking business—a fresh example of the savagery and violence that seemed to be descending on the world—and for the Schutzbund men it was a hopeless fight. One position after another was abandoned; many of the Schutzbund leaders finally got away across the border into Czechoslovakia; the resistance came to an end after the loss of, perhaps, a thousand lives.

With artillery and machineguns Dollfuss and the Heimwehr had smashed the Schutzbund; they had broken the back of the workers' organizations and presently they outlawed the Social Democratic party altogether. But they had broken something else in Austria as well. This civil war in February, 1934, was never forgotten. Never afterward was it possible to unite a great majority of Austrians behind the government which had turned its guns on the houses of the Vienna workers. Underneath, Austria was weaker and more divided than ever; and whenever a real threat should come, those who were guiding her destinies would find none behind them strong enough to defend her.

The wreckage of the battle was cleared away; the holes torn in the workers' tenements by the artillery were repaired and the marks of the machinegun bullets on their walls were plastered over. Then on the first of May Dollfuss abolished Austria's republican constitution and proclaimed in its place a "Christian dictatorship"—a curious form of government, actually a good deal like Mussolini's Fascist state in Italy, but taking its principles from the social and economic teachings of the Catholic Church. At home it relied upon the Heimwehr and upon the conservative and Catholic elements in the country. Abroad, it relied chiefly upon Italy. Italians and Austrians have often been enemies and have never had much liking for each other. But Dollfuss knew that if he was to preserve his country from the Nazis he would have to have outside help; and Mussolini had no wish to see Germany take Austria and send German armies to stand upon his own northern frontier. A group of trade treaties (they were called the "Rome protocols") was negotiated among Italy, Austria and Hungary; they reduced the tariff barriers between these states, made it a little easier for them to live and trade and tended to bring them together into a stronger defensive association. But at best it was a pretty patchwork arrangement to hold together the keystone of the European system. The Nazis were still flooding Austria with propaganda and agitation; Germany was a great and powerful nation, and if Mussolini should ever get tired of propping up Dollfuss' Christian dictatorship, it might collapse very quickly. It was at about this time that France began voting large extra sums for rebuilding and modernizing her armaments.

In the spring of 1934, however, the Nazis were finding a good deal at home to occupy them. Hitler's revolution had succeeded; he and his party were in complete control of Germany. But they had made all sorts of glowing promises, and the public was beginning to wonder whether it was not time for these promises to be made good. There was grumbling in the country. There was even grumbling within the party. It was still called the National Socialist party; Hitler had mixed up a good many socialistic ideas in its original program, and there were many radical young men among its rank and file. There was a good deal of truth in the joke that the Nazis were like an underdone beefsteak—brown on the outside but red in the middle. Talk began to be heard, that spring, about a "second revolution" which would overthrow the capitalists and reactionaries as the first had smashed the Marxists. But Hitler, who was still relying on the money and support of the wealthy and conservative classes, had no intention of making a second revolution against them—not then.

There were other troubles. There was jealousy between the Nazi storm-troop army, commanded by one of Hitler's oldest friends, Captain Ernst Röhm, and the old German regular army, whose high officers looked down on the upstart crowd of Nazi leaders and their brown-shirted gangs of street fighters. At a good many points there was a sense of strain and dissatisfaction in Germany that spring; and when another campaign of mass propaganda, parades and meetings was tried, it did not seem to help much. Various small signs suggested that an obscure crisis was approaching. But the outside world knew little of this when abruptly, on the afternoon of Saturday, June 30, huge headlines all round the earth shouted the news that many—no one knew how many—of the highest leaders of the Nazi party and of other prominent Germans had been seized and summarily shot.

Even now no one knows exactly what happened, or exactly why. No one knows whether there really was a plot against Hitler, or whether he merely imagined it, or whether there were more complicated reasons. It is supposed that the final plans were made by Hitler and Goering, his big, brutal but on the whole conservative chief lieutenant, when they flew together from Berlin to Essen on Thursday, June 28. Goering went back to Berlin, apparently to give the orders and to take charge of what was to be done there. On Friday Hitler summoned Goebbels, his acid and twisted little chief propagandist, to Essen— many believe he did so in order to protect Goebbels' life—and late that night the two men roared off in a

plane for Munich. They were there in the dawn of
Saturday. With a detachment of Hitler's special
black-uniformed SS men, or bodyguards, they drove
to the country house where Captain Röhm and other
high officers of the brown-shirt army were collected.
for a week-end party. These startled men were
dragged half awake out of their beds; Hitler raged
at them as traitors and criminals; one at least was
killed on the spot when he tried to resist. The others
were hurried to prison in Munich where most of
them died before firing squads in the course of the
day.

In Berlin at the same time and at other places the
SS men and the secret police were also busy. Many
of the victims were carried to prison and given the
form, at least, of a legal execution, but not all of
them. An automobile filled with men in plain clothes
drove up to the house of General Schleicher, who
had been Chancellor of Germany little more than a
year before. When the general and his wife came
together in answer to the doorbell both were shot
dead where they stood, and the automobile roared
away in perfect imitation of the worst kind of gang
murder. Two assistants of von Papen, who as Vice-
Chancellor still held the second-highest office in the
Cabinet, were shot; von Papen himself was arrested
and probably barely escaped with his life. It was
finally admitted officially that some fifty people were
murdered or summarily executed in this way, while
most believe that the true number of victims ran into

the hundreds at least. They seemed to be of all sorts, representing every kind of possible opposition to the dictatorship—Röhm and his storm-troop commanders, radical Nazis, conservatives like Schleicher who had opposed Hitler, Catholic leaders, the aids of von Papen, the clever intriguer. All of them were simply wiped out, suddenly, with pistols or by rifle squads. A world already shocked by the violence of the Paris riots and the savagery of the civil war in Austria was appalled to see the government of one of its greatest and most civilized nations suppressing possible opposition by the methods of gangster massacre.

The "blood purge" of June, 1934, horrified every thoughtful student of affairs and seemed to drag Europe and the world down only deeper into a swamp of force, violence and barbarism. But it left Adolf Hitler in unshakable power over 66,000,000 Germans; it consolidated the Nazi dictatorship and it freed his hands for the next move he might care to make upon the international stage. What at first looked like that next move came almost at once.

In February, Dollfuss and the Heimwehr had smashed the Austrian Social Democrats. About one o'clock in the afternoon of July 25 those who were listening to the Vienna radio heard an announcer's excited voice break into the program to declare that Dollfuss and his government had resigned and that Anton Rintelen, a prominent Austrian closely connected with the Austrian Nazis, had become Chancellor. Had the Nazis in turn made their "putsch," and had it succeeded?

Dollfuss had not resigned; but at the moment the little man was lying on the floor of his own office, slowly bleeding to death. Europe had still another shocking act of violence before it. What had happened was that a little after noon fourteen armed men had suddenly stormed into the Vienna radio station, seized it and forced the announcer to make his statement at the point of a pistol. At the same time several trucks loaded with Austrian Nazis, many of them in police or military uniforms, drove up to the Chancellery building where Dollfuss had been holding a cabinet meeting. Though the authorities had received several warnings of a plot earlier in the day, they had not increased the guards; the Nazis got into the building without trouble, swung the big doors to behind them, and, breaking up into several groups, ranged through the place, driving everyone they found as prisoners into the courtyard. One detachment, led by a former army sergeant-major, broke into the office where Dollfuss was standing. The sergeant-major raised his pistol and fired twice; the "Vest-Pocket Chancellor" staggered backward and collapsed upon the floor.

The Nazis seem to have left him lying there and started to work the telephone. They now held the radio station and the Chancellery; they had shot the Chancellor and captured several high officials. From the radio station an alarm had been sent to the police,

and a battle was raging there; around the Chancellery, however, everything was quiet and there was
nothing to show what was going on inside. But the
plot fell through. Rintelen, who was to have been
made Chancellor, seems to have lost his nerve; the
men in the Chancellery could not get in touch with
him. The authorities at last woke up. A provisional
government, under a new Chancellor, Kurt von
Schuschnigg, was set up in the War Office; police
and troops were despatched to surround the Chancellery, where the Nazis were now standing uncer-
tainly at the windows, ignorant of what was going
on outside. Someone in the meanwhile had at last
picked up Dollfuss and laid him on a sofa, where,
without even a doctor being called in, his life slowly
bled away through the long afternoon. Not until
evening were the Nazi conspirators convinced that
their attempt was a hopeless failure; and on a promise
that they would be sent safely to Germany they
came out and surrendered. By that time Dollfuss was
dead. The government on its side violated its promise, arrested the conspirators and later hanged some
of them. For two or three days afterward there were
riots and street battles in other parts of Austria, but
they were all put down; the Nazi putsch had not
succeeded, and Schuschnigg became the next regular
Chancellor of Austria. No one could know then that
he was also to be the last.

The attempt was not really a move of Hitler's; or
at least, not one which he was ready to carry through

against difficulties. It was organized by the Austrian Nazis, and by the German Nazis in Munich who supplied them with guidance, money and encouragement. Hitler had done nothing to prevent it, as he easily could have done; but he left himself free to claim afterward that the responsibility was not his. He was not yet ready to take risks—and the risks were still great. There were not only the French with their army to insist that Germany and Austria should never be united, but there was also Mussolini, who at the first news of the attempt at once ordered troops to the Austrian frontier as a plain sign that he would not permit it either. Again Europe had been shocked and shaken by a barbarous piece of bloodshed, but again the situation had been saved.

Yet it seemed that it had only just been saved; and even this tragedy was not to be the end. The French by this time were seriously worried. Under their vigorous Foreign Minister, Louis Barthou, they were trying hard to rebuild their system of alliances in Eastern Europe. They were pressing the plan of bringing Soviet Russia back into the European system as a possible ally against Germany; and in September Russia—Red Russia, whom the rest had for so long feared and hated—formally took her seat as a full member of the League of Nations. The French were seeking to come to an agreement with Mussolini for the protection of Austria against the Nazis. As a part of the plan they were trying to establish better relations between Italy and their ally, Yugoslavia; wherever they could, they were attempting to build all the rival European states back into a combination strong enough to hold Germany in check and keep the peace.

In October King Alexander of Yugoslavia arrived at Marseilles, to begin a state visit to France in promotion of these negotiations. He was received by M. Barthou, and the two men were riding away in the same car through the cheering streets when a man suddenly broke through the police line, dodged the cavalry escort, jumped on the running board of the car and emptied a submachinegun at the King. Alexander was killed instantly and Barthou, who had been struck accidentally, died a little later. So here was still another shock, not only in the barbarous fact of the assassination itself but in the example it gave of the bitterness and complexity of the quarrels which were keeping the European peoples apart. The assassin was a Yugoslav terrorist traveling on a Hungarian passport; he had apparently come from a kind of terrorist center which Hungary had allowed to be established on her own territory, and with which Italy seemed to have some connection. It unloosed new angers and suspicions; and Barthou, the ablest of the men who had been hoping to put together a working combination for peace, was dead.

There were other troubles. Far away in Spain a rebellion of radical elements had broken out against the conservative government which had recently come to power, and the government was suppressing it with a ferocious savagery. Spain, tucked away at the southwest corner of the Continent, did not seem to have much to do with the main European problems, and the rebellion was soon put down. But it deepened the general air of bloodshed and violence into which Europe was sinking, and it left memories behind it which were one day to have a great deal to do with the rest of Europe. And finally, just as this terrible year was running out, there came another episode far off in a desert of East Africa—so remote and seeming so trivial in itself that it was barely noticed in the world's great newspapers, but an episode out of which the final crash of post-war Europe was to come. At a tiny place called Walwal—a mere watering hole in the hot and empty southern desert that separated Ethiopia, the last independent native kingdom in Africa, from the Italian colony of Somaliland—there was an obscure battle on December 7 between an outpost of Italian troops and a wandering detachment of Ethiopians. The Italians called up a tank and a few airplanes and the Ethiopians were routed with great loss. It seemed just an unimportant border dispute; it was actually the first battle of a war which was to shake what was left of the European system into bits.

6. SOMETHING FOR SOMETHING

ON THE EVENING OF JANUARY 3, 1935, M. Pierre Laval, the Premier of France and Foreign Minister as well since the assassination of M. Barthou, was taking the train for Rome for an interview with Premier Mussolini. The papers being sold through the station as he left carried the news that the Emperor Haile Selassie of Ethiopia had appealed that day to the League of Nations, reporting the Walwal battle as a case of Italian aggression involving a threat of war against Ethiopia, which was a member of the League. M. Laval probably did not think this matter of much importance. The swarthy, stocky French politician, with shrewd and very practical eyes, was on his way to Rome to make a trade which would have very little to do with the ideals of the League of Nations.

Since the end of the World War the Italians, who felt that they had been cheated out of their rightful gains by the peace treaties, had been quarreling with the French and encouraging the Germans. Now, however, that the Germans under Hitler were again

becoming really powerful, Mussolini was beginning
to find them almost as dangerous as they seemed to
the French. M. Laval was now going to Rome to see
whether he could not settle the disputes between
France and Italy and secure Mussolini as an ally who
would help hold the Germans in check. The negotiations lasted two or three days, and at the end there
was a formal statement of the usual sort, declaring
that the issues between the two powers had been settled and announcing various small concessions—
dealing with colonial readjustments in Africa—which
France would make to Italy. But the concessions
were so unimportant that it seemed as if M. Laval
must have given Mussolini something besides which
was not announced. Most people believe that either
directly or indirectly he did so; and that the something was Ethiopia.

Few knew it at the time, but Mussolini had already
decided that he was going to conquer that backward,
still largely barbaric, African empire in a deliberate
war of aggression. He had many reasons for this
adventure of the "practical" and brutal sort which
seem sufficient to the new dictatorial governments
such as he had established. He wanted to increase
Italian prestige in the world by fighting a successful
war and seizing his own share of African empire,
just as the other powers had done in the century
before. He wanted to arouse the patriotic enthusiasm
of his own people and give them something to take
their minds off the economic depression and their

grumblings against his régime. He believed that in Ethiopia he might actually find enough raw materials, enough new markets and enough land for Italian settlement to be of some help in meeting Italy's very real economic needs. He thought the war could be won without killing very many Italians, and he cared nothing about killing Ethiopians. He cared just as little about democratic ideas of peace, of international law and of putting down aggression; and the fact that he was bound, since both Ethiopia and Italy were members of the League, to respect Ethiopia's territory and independence, meant nothing to him. He had begun quite seriously and deliberately to prepare his conquest as far back as 1933, in the depths of the world depression; and he had already decided, at the time M. Laval arrived in Rome, that the attack must be made in the following autumn. The fight at Walwal was in fact a part of the general scheme of aggression, and Haile Selassie had every reason to appeal urgently to the League.

But M. Laval, on his side, was not thinking about the League or its obligations; he was thinking, and also in a very "practical" way, about the growing menace from Germany. It made little difference to France if Mussolini wanted to occupy himself with a picturesque war in this out-of-the-way corner of Africa; M. Laval cared as little for the Ethiopians as Mussolini did, and if he could enlist Mussolini as an ally against the Germans simply by telling him that France would not interfere with the Ethiopian adventure, it would be a cheap bargain. M. Laval went home. The Italians presently consulted the British government; the British were too careful to make any definite promises, but their diplomatic officials apparently decided that Ethiopia meant as little to them as it seems to have meant to M. Laval. They, too, were thinking about Germany. Mussolini, thus led to believe that there would be no trouble from France or Great Britain, went busily ahead with his preparations, sending out supplies and troops to his colonies of Eritrea and Somaliland, which bordered on Ethiopia, and instructing his representatives at Geneva to make sure that the League of Nations did nothing of importance to help Haile Selassie.

Matters were at this stage when Hitler suddenly gave France and Britain something very serious to think about. With the agreement, in January, between France and Italy, the British and French diplomats had begun to entertain all sorts of high hopes of bringing Hitler to a definite settlement which would re-establish peace in Europe. Early in February they had even made Hitler a formal offer of a "freely negotiated" agreement. It was to include treaties in which the various powers would guarantee the frontiers in Eastern Europe just as they had guaranteed the western frontier of Germany in the Locarno pacts; with that done, the former Allies would agree to abolish the disarmament clauses of the Versailles treaty if Germany would enter into a new arms limitation treaty to be negotiated with her as an equal. What this really meant was that the former Allies would do away with the appearance of compulsory, one-sided disarmament if Hitler would promise to accept the general situation as it existed, and not go too far in building up the new armaments which everyone pretty well knew by this time that he was secretly acquiring.

Hitler's answer to this was bold and abrupt. On March 10, General Goering made it known in a newspaper interview that Germany was already building the military air force which was forbidden to her by the Versailles treaty. Nothing much happened; and on Saturday, March 16, this trial shot was followed by a bombshell. Hitler announced to the world, in effect, that he had abolished the disarmament clauses of the Versailles treaty himself. Without asking French, British or Italian leave, universal military service had been re-established and a peacetime army of thirty-six divisions set up. "The memory," said a Nazi manifesto, "of the glorious German army with its glorious history is now no longer a pale historic phantom." Hitler himself coupled this pronouncement with a pledge that he wanted nothing but peace; he had no more territorial claims on France; he had offered nonaggression pacts to all his neighbors; he gave his assurance that he did not intend "in rearming Germany to create any instrument for warlike attack, but, on the contrary, exclusively for defense and thereby for the maintenance of peace." But he left no doubt that he would rearm Germany as rapidly and as heavily as he pleased.

The French were furious; the Italians were only less so; the British were alarmed, but indecisive. The French appealed to the League of Nations and fired a vigorous protest at Berlin against this violation of treaties; the Italians—who were at that very moment preparing a war of conquest against a fellow member of the League in violation of all their own treaty obligations—did the same. But the British were inclined to feel that they should try to make the best of what couldn't be helped. If the others were not too severe about Germany's action, Hitler might yet be brought to sign agreements limiting the extent of his rearmament and really guaranteeing the frontiers in Eastern Europe. The diplomats rushed frantically around from one capital to another; the British even went as far as Moscow, which most of them still distrusted rather more than they distrusted Hitler; but nothing happened. Finally, the French and the British and the Italians all met on Isola Bella—a little island off Stresa, in Lake Maggiore—and talked over the crisis for three days. They ended with a set of resolutions in which they scolded Germany, promised to work for a settlement in Eastern Europe, promised to consult if there were any threat to Austrian independence, promised to go on with the attempt to secure disarmament—and, in short, made it clear that they intended to do nothing. The second of Hitler's bold strokes had proved, like the first,* a brilliant success. And the second of the three main pillars on which the post-war European system had been built had crashed to the ground. The first, the reparations settlement, had fallen in June, 1931. The military clauses of the Versailles treaty and the enforced disarmament of Germany were now only a memory. It was time to ask how long the third pillar—the territorial and political settlements—could hope to stand.

In the meanwhile, Haile Selassie, unluckily choosing the very day after Hitler exploded his bombshell, had made a second appeal to the League of Nations, pointing to the continued arrival of Italian troops in East Africa and the danger that Ethiopia was about to be attacked. At their meeting near Stresa the French, British and Italians had also resolved that their policy was "the maintenance of peace within the framework of the League of Nations." But no one supposed that would apply to Ethiopia; or if any of them did, they were careful not to think about it. The French and British knew that the "Stresa Front"—as this agreement was called —was feeble enough as a defense against the German threat, without raising any difficulties about Mussolini's ambitions in Africa. Mussolini went on massing his troops. The French and the British turned, each in their own way, to protect themselves further against the new problem created by German rearmament; and in doing so, they only made clearer than

* See page 105.

before how much uncertainty, how much division of policy, how much disunion there was among the great Western powers.

The British still felt that if they were careful not to annoy him, Hitler would come to a reasonable policy; and they succeeded in making a naval agreement with him under which he promised that in re-armament at sea he would not go beyond 35 per cent of the British Navy. This was an easy promise for Hitler to make. It would have taken him years under any circumstances to build beyond that limit, and for the moment he would be fully occupied with the more important job of building up his army to match that of France. Still, the agreement reassured the British; but it exasperated the French, as they felt that the British had let them down.

The French on their part turned back to their old idea of securing Soviet Russia as a military ally. Hitler, throughout his whole rise to power and since he had taken office, had never ceased to hold up Russian Bolshevism as the great enemy of civilization; and he and his lieutenants were constantly attacking the Soviets or hinting at vast plans for conquering territory from them in language which gave the secretive people in the Kremlin plenty of reason to fear the Germans. The Russians were willing to join with the French, and in May two treaties were signed (though not finally ratified) which were later on to be of great importance. One was a treaty of mutual assistance between France and Russia, under which the two countries agreed, in effect, that if either was attacked by Germany the other would come to its aid. The second was a treaty of mutual assistance between Russia and Czechoslovakia, France's small ally. Again, each agreed to come to the other's aid in the event of an attack by Germany, but only if France, in accordance with the first treaty, did the same. A look at the map will show why the Czech treaty was important. The Russian border nowhere touched the German; but Czechoslovakia was a kind of bridge over which Russian airplanes or even (if Rumania assented) Russian troops could be brought almost into the heart of Germany. The Germans, naturally, were angry. But these treaties did not particularly please the British, either, who feared and disliked the Bolshevists; and they pleased Mussolini, who like Hitler had built his whole career on fighting Russian Communism, even less.

Thus the Stresa Front was weak enough at best. But it was only as the summer went on, as Mussolini got nearer and nearer to his date for opening the war on Ethiopia and as Ethiopia's appeals to the League became more and more urgent, that the really disastrous character of its weakness began to appear. The post-war European system had been founded on the three pillars of reparations, German disarmament and the territorial revisions; it had been completed by setting the League of Nations at the top of the structure to hold it together and to correct any dangers that might appear. It is true that the League had never been of much practical effect, and the politicians and diplomats seldom paid much attention to it except when they thought they could use it for their own special ends. But all of them gave it lip service; most of them declared that their policy was based on their League obligations, and most of them wanted to preserve it with the idea that some day it might prove to be their best defense against aggression and another great war. Now that Hitler Germany had kicked over two of the foundation pillars of the post-war system and the danger of a great war was every day becoming more serious, could the French and British allow the League to be destroyed and so let one of the most important parts of their post-war system go to smash just when it might be most needed?

The system was being directly threatened by Germany. The easiest and most practical way of suppressing Germany had seemed to be to bring the Italians over to the French and British side. But Italy was a dictatorship very much like the German; Mussolini was violent, militarist, and as contemptuous of the League as Hitler was; he was plotting a small aggressive war of his own and was quite as much a threat to the system in his own way as were the Germans. The Allies' trouble was that by keeping Italian friendship they might suppress Germany, but they would have to reduce the League to a sham. If they remained true to the League and therefore to the whole system they were trying to defend, they would lose Italy as an ally and be unable to put down the German threat. And that wasn't the worst of it. As the war danger had increased over the past few years, the British government in particular had more and more firmly promised the British people that it would work for peace through standing by the League. In an unexpected way Mussolini's Ethiopian adventure was showing just how complicated a business that was going to be and how deep was the real sickness at the heart of the whole European community. Under the circumstances the professional politicians and diplomats of France and England would probably have preferred to make sure of Mussolini and to forget the League; they would probably have been willing to let him have his war. But their peoples—and especially the British people—were not.

As spring gave way to summer, as a steadily growing procession of Italian transports was seen passing through the Suez Canal, carrying whole divisions of troops to Eritrea and Italian Somaliland, as Haile Selassie's appeals became more urgent, world opinion paid less and less attention to the great effort of rearmament being pushed furiously forward in Germany and became more and more absorbed in the remarkable proceedings going on in East Africa. The League of Nations at Geneva had begun by trying simply to put off the whole problem in the hope that it might somehow cure itself. But with Mussolini now making belligerent speeches to his soldiers, hinting

that he was sending them upon a glorious war of conquest—in flagrant violation of everything which the
League was supposed to stand for—that policy became more and more difficult.

Public opinion in Great Britain began to be thoroughly aroused. It had been taught to believe that its
government's policy was to work for world peace by
supporting the League. During the winter and spring
League advocates in Great Britain had been carrying
on a remarkable nation-wide straw poll. Out of a
total of 11,500,000 persons who cast ballots, 11,000,-
000 voted that Great Britain should continue to be a
member of the League; 10,000,000 voted that in the
event of a war of aggression Great Britain should join
with other nations in taking economic measures
against the aggressor; while no less than 6,785,000
voted for taking military measures as well if those
should be necessary. Mr. Stanley Baldwin, the Prime
Minister, and his Conservative cabinet ministers were
thoroughly alarmed by such signs as this of the attitude of the British public. They were afraid that if
they simply dropped the League overboard they
would be thrown out of office; and they were afraid
that if they took the lead at Geneva in securing
League measures to stop Mussolini they would only
bring on themselves a bloody war with the dictator
—a war which nobody wanted and of which Herr
Hitler would be the chief beneficiary. Not knowing
what to do, Mr. Baldwin tried a policy of half-heartedly attempting to do everything at the same time.

Together with the French, he tried to buy off Mussolini by various offers of minor concessions. Ethiopia would be induced to turn over some of her less valuable territory to Italy, to give economic rights to the Italians and allow them to build a new railroad across Ethiopia; Great Britain would even help out by offering to Ethiopia a strip of her own British Somaliland in return. Mussolini contemptuously waved aside all such small change as that. Mr. Baldwin tried hinting at the use of force, and in September the large British Mediterranean Fleet was heavily reinforced with ships brought even from as far away as China. The Italians answered by declaring that if they were interfered with they would · bomb the British squadrons without hesitation. The League was assembled at Geneva to consider the whole Ethiopian problem; Mussolini let it be known that he was going ahead anyway "with Geneva, without Geneva, against Geneva" if necessary. The supporters of the League in Great Britain insisted that all this was just bluff, and that with really determined action—such as the imposing of economic embargoes on Italy and the closing of the Suez Canal —not only would it be impossible for Mussolini to wage his war in Ethiopia, but he would never dare to go to war with Britain. As if accepting this view, Mr. Baldwin allowed his Foreign Minister, Sir Samuel Hoare, to make a famous speech at Geneva on September 11, 1935. "The League stands," Sir Samuel declared, "and my country stands with it, for the

collective maintenance of the Covenant in its entirety
and particularly for steady and collective resistance
to all acts of unprovoked aggression."

It sounded very impressive. But if Mussolini was
bluffing—and no doubt he was—this was pure bluff
on the other side. Indeed, the day before Sir Samuel
spoke he had privately agreed with M. Laval that
whatever France and Britain did, they would take
no military measures against Italy, they would not
close the Suez Canal, they would, "in a word," rule
out "everything that might lead to war." If the two
chief League powers were resolved not even to risk
a war, it is clear that they had no means of stopping
Mussolini except by bluff. But the Italian dictator was
a far better bluffer than Mr. Baldwin. The game
would have been ridiculous if it had not been so tragic
—for Ethiopia, and even more for Europe, whose
one great agency for maintaining peace, order and
international law was now facing its decisive test.

The League bluff went on. There were more com-
mittees, more attempts to find some "formula" that
would satisfy the Italians, more reports accomplishing nothing. Matters were still in this stage when
Mussolini's scheduled date arrived. Suddenly, on
October 2, there was a national mobilization in Italy;
from the balcony of his office in Rome Mussolini
was giving a fiery speech to a vast throng assembled
in the square outside, and early on the following
morning scattered lines of Italian skirmishers were
scrambling down the wild slopes of the gorge of the

Mareb River—the boundary between Eritrea and Ethiopia—splashing through the water and clambering up the ridges on the Ethiopian side. The popping of rifle fire here and there around the few weak Ethiopian frontier posts soon ceased. The invasion had begun. Mussolini's war was a fact. What was the world, or the League of Nations, going to do about it?

The net result of the excitement, the confusion and the tragic absurdities which followed was that the League, and the world, did nothing effective. The trouble was that the League had already gone so far that it could not afford—as would probably have been better for everyone, including the Ethiopians—to do nothing at all. For years supporters of the League had been arguing that its machinery could not be called a failure because it had never been tried. Here at last a crisis had arrived. If the machinery were not tried now, it would amount to a confession that it never could be tried and the failure would be complete. But it seemed likely that if the machinery were tried it was bound to fail anyway. The solution which the statesmen of the chief League powers found for this dilemma was to put the machinery into operation—but only half-heartedly.

The League Council met and formally adjudged Italy an aggressor. To the fifty member nations of the League it recommended the economic "sanctions"—that is to say, the export and import embargoes—which they should impose on Italy in order to bring the aggression to a halt. But it avoided recommending the one measure, an embargo on the export of coal and oil and gasoline to Italy, which might really have compelled Mussolini to end the war. The effect was to irritate the Italians to the last pitch of anger and exasperation against the League and against the French and British, without putting any serious difficulty in the way of their conquest of Ethiopia. It was not until the middle of November that even these sanctions actually went into effect. By that time the Italian armies were getting deep into the deserts and the wild mountain uplands of Ethiopia. Haile Selassie had concentrated his hordes of half-barbarian, badly armed soldiery to oppose them, but Ethiopia's chances at best were not bright.

The French and British diplomats, alarmed lest public opinion should force them to go on and impose an oil embargo on Italy, saw that the prompt end of the war was the simplest way out of their difficulties and were busily engaged in bringing the Ethiopian Emperor to make peace on any terms. It was at this point that Sir Samuel Hoare, on his way to a vacation in the Swiss Alps, stopped off in Paris to see M. Laval. The two statesmen agreed on a peace plan which they thought was the best, as a practical matter, that they could hope to get both Mussolini and Haile Selassie to accept. It amounted to handing over about half of Ethiopia to the Italians and leaving what remained completely under Italian domination—in other words, to ending a brazen aggression by handsomely rewarding the aggressor and giving him most of what he wanted from the victim. Sir Samuel, apparently not appreciating what violence this would do to the whole idea of League action against aggression, which his government was still pretending to support, went contentedly on to enjoy the winter sports in Switzerland. Unfortunately, this peace plan —the "Hoare-Laval plan," as it was afterwards known —leaked out to the newspapers only a day or two later. It created a terrific scandal.

Liberal and pro-League opinion in Great Britain was shocked, horrified and outraged by the seemingly brutal cynicism of this proposal to abandon everything which the League was supposed to be standing for, and to put down what was being pictured as highway robbery by bestowing half the contents of the victim's pocket on the robber. Actually, the Hoare-Laval plan probably did represent the best and least unjust solution which, under all the circumstances, there was any possibility of achieving by that time. But the storm of popular disapproval which greeted it forced Sir Samuel out of the Foreign Office, forced M. Laval to resign, and effectually killed the plan. The Italian armies went methodically ahead, throwing back the offensives attempted against them by the Ethiopians and building roads, perfecting supply systems and otherwise preparing for the final blows which were mercilessly to crush the Ethiopian armies and shatter their semibarbaric empire. Sir Samuel's successor, the young, popular and handsome Mr. Anthony Eden, went through the motions about the oil embargo. The motions were as futile as those which had gone before, and with as little conviction behind them; and in the end Mr. Eden, who had taken office as an idealistic supporter of the League who might really make it work, found that his actual task was to bury the whole business more cynically and more completely than would have been done under the Hoare-Laval plan itself.

Meanwhile the democratic world watched with a deepening sense of horror and disgust as the Italian aviation ranged over Ethiopia (the Ethiopians had no airplanes and no anti-aircraft artillery with which to oppose it), bombing the mud-hut towns and villages of the empire or spraying the ground with mustard gas which burned the bare feet and seared the bodies of the helpless population. Though it had seen the beginning of horrors of the same sort in the Japanese invasion of Manchuria and at Shanghai, the world was not as used to this sort of thing as it was later on to become, and it seemed a shocking business. But the Italians went systematically ahead. In three pitched battles, between February 10 and March 4, 1936, they attacked the three main Ethiopian armies, surrounding each one in turn, pounding down its sturdy resistance with artillery and air bombing to which the Ethiopians had no means of replying, and then turning the resultant retreat into a terrible rout by sending in aviation to slaughter the escaping troops in thousands. Only one last important army, led by Emperor Haile Selassie himself, remained to oppose the Italian advance upon the Ethiopian capital, Addis Ababa. Knowing that he was probably lost whatever he did, the Emperor decided to gamble on an attack against the Italian forces before him. He sent a wireless message (which the Italians intercepted and read, thus being put on their guard) to his Empress:

> Since our faith rests in our Creator and in the hope that He will aid us, having decided to advance . . . confide in secret this our decision to the ministers and dignitaries, and address your prayers to God.

But God could help him as little as the League of Nations. The attack was delivered on March 31, with great courage and ferocity, but it shattered itself upon the Italian machineguns; when the day was over nothing had been gained, and there was no course but to order a retreat. As the Ethiopians streamed away from the scene, the terrible air bombs rained down upon them; once more retreat became a rout, and the Emperor's army melted away to nothing. Haile Selassie managed to escape; but all hope of resistance was over. The Italians threw forward a fast motorized column to cover the 250 miles which still separated them from Addis Ababa. The Emperor reached his capital ahead of them and made some attempts to organize a last resistance, but his government was already going to pieces around him and it was clearly useless.

On May 2 he left with his family for the coast while there was still time; behind him a wild orgy of riot and looting broke out in the demoralized city, and when the Italians—implored to hurry by the foreign residents who were trapped there—entered Addis Ababa early on May 5 it was under a pall of smoke rising from the wrecked and blazing ruin which was all that remained of the capital of Haile Selassie, last emperor of the last native kingdom in Africa. Mussolini's war was over. He had his glorious conquest, in spite of Britain, of France and of all fifty powers in the League of Nations. But long before that, something else had happened which had left Britain and France very little time or inclination to think about Ethiopia.

The main Italian attack had got under way, as has been said, in the second week of February. But the British, the French, the other League powers, were not the only ones who were watching its progress or drawing their own conclusions from the strange tragi-comedy revolving around Ethiopia's fate. It was not lost on Adolf Hitler that the Stresa Front, which had been formed against him when he had announced Germany's rearmament in the preceding March, was now shattered beyond repair, with two of its members—Italy and Great Britain—much nearer to war with each other than they were to undertaking a war against Germany, with many of the French irritated at the British for dragging them into what they felt to be the foolish business of League sanctions, and with many of the British irritated at the French for doing everything, as the British thought, to make sure that the sanctions would be ineffective. The futility of the League system for keeping peace did not escape him. The general confusion, uncertainty and cross-purposes of democratic policy had been brilliantly illuminated. The opportunity that all this presented him for still another stroke, even bolder than that of a year ago, was plain. Some hints that something might be coming were reaching French and British ears, and they may have helped to secure, on February 27, the ratification by the French Chamber of the treaty of mutual assistance with Soviet Russia which had been signed in May.* But neither France nor Britain was prepared for what did come, again with the suddenness of a thunderbolt, on Saturday, March 7.

There had been a cabinet meeting in Berlin the evening before; at its conclusion it was announced that Hitler's tame Reichstag would meet at noon next day to hear an address by the Chancellor, while the foreign ambassadors were asked to come to the Foreign Office in the morning. They duly arrived, to be told by the German Foreign Minister that at dawn that day German troops had rumbled across the Rhine bridges into the zone between the river and

* See page 132.

the French border which had been forever demilitarized by the Versailles treaty and guaranteed by the Locarno pacts.* At the same time they were handed a long note, announcing that Germany would no longer be bound by her signature to the Locarno treaties and would do as she pleased in the demilitarized zone.

There was a great deal else in the note. There was a long series of proposals for new treaties of peace, of nonaggression and of general settlement. There was an elaborate excuse for the violation of the Locarno pact. According to this argument, the French, by ratifying their treaty for a military alliance with Soviet Russia, had changed the whole situation on which the Locarno agreement was based; therefore the treaty had already "lost its significance and practically ceased to be." But Hitler had made peace offers before; the legal argument about Locarno required, to say the least, a very strained interpretation of the treaty; while no amount of argument could conceal the essentials of what had happened.

Hitler had simply torn up a solemn treaty obligation without notice and without hesitation. It is true that he had done so before in the case of the Versailles treaty clauses; but he had always refused to regard the Versailles treaty as binding, because Germany had signed it only under compulsion, and many in Great Britain and France had been inclined to

* See pages 10 and 57.

feel the same way about it. Here, however, he had torn up a treaty which Germany had negotiated and signed of her own free will. But, much more than that, this particular treaty which he had destroyed was the last and most important defense of the postwar world. So long as Germany's western frontier remained unfortified, Hitler could make no move in any direction except under the immediate threat of invasion by the French Army. The independence of Austria, the safety of Czechoslovakia and Poland and in large measure of Rumania and Yugoslavia, the whole territorial settlement of Versailles and the balance built up upon it, all depended in the last analysis upon the fact that if necessary the French could always march into Germany. But once the western frontier was walled up with troops and fortresses, France would no longer be able to come readily to the aid of her small allies in the east; her power of protecting them would be largely lost; Germany would be set free for almost any adventure, and the post-war system would be at an end.

The three pillars of that system were the reparations, the military and the territorial settlements. Two of them had gone already; Hitler was now knocking the largest foundation stone from under the third. His speech to the Reichstag that Saturday noon was full of promises: "Now, more than ever we shall strive for an understanding between European peoples. . . . We have no territorial demands to make in Europe. . . . I now ask the German people . . .

especially to support me in my struggle for real peace." He used the Franco-Russian treaty for all it was worth, justifying his own action on the ground that he was saving Europe from Bolshevism. "I will not have the gruesome Communist international dictatorship of hate descend upon the German people." But he was emphatic: "We swear to yield to no force whatever . . . and prefer to succumb . . . rather than to capitulate."

As Hitler's frenzied oratory thundered through the loudspeakers, columns of German troops were rolling on across the Rhine bridges, spreading steadily through the demilitarized zone. They were not in great force. It is now believed that the German General Staff had advised Hitler against the adventure on the ground that it was too dangerous, and that the troops were under orders to withdraw at once if they met opposition from France. But there was no opposition from France. The hours went by. The last pillar of the post-war system was crumbling to collapse under the German army boots; the last moment at which that system might, perhaps, have been saved in its essentials had arrived. And the great democracies which had created it did nothing.

They did not know what to do. They did not want to risk a war. They did not know how far Hitler was making a colossal bluff. The British had no desire to get involved in an invasion of Germany. The French did not want to act without full support from Great Britain. Many British argued that Germany had a right to fortify her own territory anyway. The horrors of war seemed certain and immediate; what Hitler would actually do with the freedom he was seizing was uncertain and remote. It seemed better to do nothing reckless and hope for the best. The French announced that their army would not march; but that they would appeal to the League of Nations. Mr. Eden, the British Foreign Secretary, declaring that "one of the main foundations of the peace of Western Europe has been cut away," lamely concluded that "if peace is to be secured there is a manifest duty to rebuild." He would start the rebuilding by considering Hitler's proffered new peace and non-aggression treaties. But the League of Nations had just been reduced to a ridiculous sham by the Ethiopian affair; and though there was to be some discussion of Hitler's peace offers, it was soon clear that nothing could be done with them.

The post-war system, as it had been painfully put together at Versailles and in the years that followed, had fallen at last and had been abandoned by its chief architects and supporters. There were few in Britain or in France who could bring themselves to believe it at the time. But still another period of European history was over. The Great War had been won in 1918. From then until 1925 the nations had been absorbed in making the peace, clearing away the wreckage and setting up a going international system under the general guidance of the victors. From about 1925 to 1930 that system had worked fairly well. But beginning with the Great Depression in 1930 it had begun to go to pieces, and from Hitler's rise to power in 1933 the collapse had been swift. Now the system was in fragments. Reparations had gone, disarmament had gone, Locarno and the French power to maintain Eastern Europe had gone, the League had gone. Whatever was to happen next, something new would have to be worked out. Some new way would have to be found of organizing the rival European peoples and regulating their relations with each other. Looking back on it now we can see that from March 7, 1936, there was really only one question that mattered. Could such a job be done without another great war?

There was a humiliating and pathetic postscript to the story of the Ethiopian War. Something still had to be done about the sanctions which the League, through its fifty members, was imposing on Italy. There were some who still tried to believe that if real sanctions, including an oil embargo, were adopted, Italy could even then be made to give up her conquest. It was a foolish notion; and at the end of June there was a shamefaced meeting of the League to bring sanctions to an end and so to admit that the whole effort to stop aggression had been a flat failure. Young Mr. Anthony Eden, who had taken office as a supporter of the League who might make it work, had to make the painful journey to Geneva to give it as decent a burial as possible. The proceedings were hurried. But there was one speaker

at the gathering to whom the whole world listened.
He was Haile Selassie, the deposed emperor of a barbarian state, but a man of dignity and self-control,
who now spoke with a great and impressive earnest-
ness:

> I pray to Almighty God that he shall spare to
> the nations the terrible sufferings that have just
> been inflicted on my people. . . . It is inter-
> national morality that is at stake. . . . Should
> it happen that a strong government finds that it
> may with impunity destroy a small people, then
> the hour strikes for that weak people to appeal
> to the League to give its judgment in all free-
> dom. God and history will remember your judg-
> ment.

The delegates of the great powers fidgeted in their
seats and of course paid no attention to the appeal.
None had paid attention to an earlier appeal of the
Emperor's, which he had sent from Addis Ababa in
the last days:

> Do the peoples of the world not yet realize
> that by fighting on until the bitter end I am . . .
> standing guard in the last citadel of collective
> security? . . . I must still hold on until my
> tardy allies appear. If they never come, then I
> say prophetically and without bitterness: "The
> West will perish."

Those words are remembered now, and some may
wonder whether they will not in the end prove

right. In the flames which greeted the Italian troops as they rolled down from the Ethiopian hills into Addis Ababa much more had perished than the ramshackle houses of a barbarian capital. And those flames were now to spread across a world.

7. SOMETHING FOR NOTHING

WHAT DO WE MEAN BY SAYING THAT a new "system" or a new order had to be created? Into the continent of Europe there was packed a whole collection of peoples, great and small, with their rival governments each claiming to be completely "sovereign," or independent of all the rest. Among them were two great democracies, France and Britain; there were now three absolute dictatorships, Russia, Italy and Germany; while grouped around these five were a score of lesser nations, some democratic, some dictatorial and others showing nearly all stages in between. All were suffering under the effects of the Great Depression; all faced serious domestic problems; none was particularly happy or prosperous and many were desperately poor.

Each government was being driven by its restless people to promise them a richer, brighter, more splendid future. Each government was trying to make good its promises by all sorts of devices—by tariffs, by subsidies, by efforts to find new markets abroad, by demands for more land or colonies, by shows and propaganda campaigns—none of which was working very well and most of which were bringing the governments closer and closer to bankruptcy. Many of these devices depended on improving the situation at home, on trying to make it possible for the nation to live better on what resources it had, and did not directly affect other nations. But many, on the other hand, brought each government into conflict with other governments which were all trying to save themselves in the same ways; while one of the easiest courses for any politician was to tell his people that their troubles really came from the injustices imposed upon them by other nations and that the true solution was for them to seize the "rights"—in more land, or more markets or greater national power—which others owed them. And all these governments now had at their command huge armies, navies and air forces, which were supposed to be purely defensive but which could be let loose at any moment in order to grab these fancied opportunities.

Each nation feared the others as it struggled to outdo them; and among them all they were only making matters worse. The armies and air forces

were growing larger every day; the peoples were becoming more restless, the gap between what they
had and what their governments promised them was
widening. Such a state of affairs could not last. All
these separate nations with their conflicting policies
and dangerous armies had to be fitted together in
some way so that all would have at least some chance
to live and prosper without threatening to destroy
the rest, and so that those who might still try to
destroy the rest would not have the power to do so.
Some method for adjusting the relations between
them would have to be found—that was inevitable.
The only question by the summer of 1936 was
whether this could still be done by diplomacy, or
whether matters had gone so far that there would
first have to be a great war to clear away the tangles
of fear and rivalry and threat that stood in the way.
The nations of Europe were like a set of knobbly
building blocks which had to be fitted together in
some arrangement that would stay put; they were
very knobbly blocks to begin with, and what made it
worse was that each building block was also a bomb
which, if it slipped, might go off and blow up all
the rest.

If we look at the five big building blocks in turn
we see first the two great democracies, France and
Britain. They were the richest and most nearly satisfied of all the European great powers. Their chief
politicians believed in peace, in capitalistic industry
and trade and democratic freedom, and they thought

that if all nations would only try to work with one another, each would come out better than any could do by its own efforts. They were afraid of two things —Communist revolution or disruption among their own people, and an attack from rearming Germany. But what they wanted above all was to be left alone.

The Soviet Russian dictatorship also claimed at that time that it wanted nothing but to be left alone to work out its own domestic problems. But it was afraid of the German Nazis, with their constant attacks on Communism and their vast plans for one day invading and annexing great sections of Russian territory. As a result, it had made the mutual assistance treaties with France and Czechoslovakia, and had ordered its followers in the Western democratic countries to form the "united front" with Left and liberal democratic parties. Fascism, the Soviets declared, was the great enemy, and Russia would work with all forces opposed to it. Yet in the capitalist democratic countries men could not forget the great dream of Communist world revolution which lay behind the Russian experiment; Russia was a dictatorship, using methods as cynical, brutal, violent and utterly undemocratic as those of the Fascists or Nazis, and there were many in the Western nations who could never feel sure that the "united front" was not simply a trick for helping Communism to come to power some day in their own countries.

The Italian dictatorship was restless and ambitious. It wanted more power, more prestige in the world;

new territories that would give it the industrial raw materials in which Italy is almost wholly lacking, and control over the entrances to the Mediterranean Sea, so that Italy would always have sure access to world supplies of those materials she could not acquire for her own. Mussolini had no patience with democratic ideas of friendly international co-operation in which all would work out their problems together. He was constantly making warlike speeches, arming Italy up to the limit she could afford and spreading the idea that what Italy was not given she would fight to take.

But Mussolini was an extremely shrewd politician who actually had no intention of getting his country into a great war. Instead, he worked for his ends by playing one set of powers against another. He encouraged Germany when Germany was weak as a means of threatening France and Britain; he stood with the French and British when Germany grew stronger, thus making himself so valuable to the democracies that they could not afford to refuse his demands. He was a dictator like Hitler and so could work easily with the Germans; at the same time, his dictatorship was less brutal and extreme than that of the Nazis, it did not threaten democratic ideas in quite so violent a way, and so Mussolini could work almost as easily with the democracies. All this made Italy one of the knobbliest and slipperiest of all the building blocks. Italy could probably have been fitted into almost any kind of pattern, once it had been worked out; but her two-sided policy added greatly to the difficulty of working out any pattern at all.

The last of the big building blocks was Nazi Germany. Adolf Hitler had now freed his country of the last restrictions of the Versailles treaty. Germany no longer had to pay reparations; she was free to arm herself as she pleased; she was free to fortify her western frontier; she had nothing to fear from the empty shell of the League of Nations. She was still comparatively poor in raw materials and in industrial markets, and her people still bitterly resented the loss of the territories and colonies that had been taken away from them in 1919. Yet it is not impossible that even these last questions could have been adjusted if Germany had now been willing to work with the other great powers in a friendly and co-operative spirit. If she had used her new liberty and power for peace, for real disarmament, for better economic arrangements in Europe and greater opportunities for all, something might, perhaps, have been done. A really working system might have been created under which not only Europe as a whole but the German people themselves would have won much more true safety and prosperity than could have been won in any other way.

But the gangster government of the Nazis had no interest in such methods. Whatever they had got from the victor powers they had got by threat, bluster and force. What they wanted for themselves was not peace; it was prestige, power and successful war.

They were making every effort to turn Germany not merely into an "armed camp," but into one vast, co-ordinated war-making machine with the single supreme purpose of winning victory on the battlefield. Their answer to every problem of the German people was that Germany must be "strong"; their solution for every want or ill under which Germans (like all other peoples) suffered was some scheme to seize land or power or opportunity from others—by threats and diplomatic maneuvers if possible; if not, by war.

Hitler and the adventurers he had gathered around him talked a great deal about peace. But they did not want merely to be let alone; they had no intention of letting other peoples alone. They were resolved upon an aggressive policy to claim the "rights" to which they had decided that Germany was entitled, and throughout all the latter part of 1936 and 1937 they were actively making ready the ground. They had a great deal to work with. They had the poverty and unrest in most of the smaller European countries, on which their propaganda could play to divide and weaken opposition to them. They had the fact that there were important German-speaking minorities in several of these states, which could be organized, just as the Nazi sympathizers in Austria had been organized, to throw the affairs of the countries in which they lived into turmoil, help to paralyze their governments and prepare the way for a later German advance. In Czechoslovakia, particularly, there were the 3,500,000 Sudeten Germans—about a quarter of the population—who lived all around the fringes of the country, thus occupying the mountainous frontier area that was vital to its defense against Germany. These people had never been a part of prewar Germany, and their local Nazi party pretended to have no connections with the German Nazis, but as it now began to clamor against the wrongs and oppressions of the Sudeten Germans and to agitate for greater freedom from the rule of the Czech and Slovak majority, it was creating the conditions necessary for the splitting up and destruction of the state.

But Hitler and his Nazis had even more than this to work with. They could make use of Italy's wavering policy for their own advantage. They had the divisions of opinion between France and Britain, the democratic reluctance to face the idea of war and the tendency of all democratic governments to put off all decisions until the last moment. And they had the paralyzing effect introduced into democratic diplomacy by the existence of Soviet Russia. There were many leaders in Britain and in France who could never make up their minds whether Bolshevist revolution at home or Nazi aggression was really the greater danger. Many of them believed Hitler's claim that he was the defender of Europe against Communism, and always hesitated to press the German dictator too hard, for fear that if he were overthrown the result would be a Communist revolution in Germany that would spread through Europe. Hitler's greatest danger was a strong alliance joining France, Britain and Russia; but he was protected against it by the democracies' fears of this "united front" which Stalin's Russia professed to hold out to them. It was hard to save the remaining democratic countries from Hitler without inviting in Communism; it was hard to save them from Communism without greatly strengthening Hitler. This was, perhaps, the most important single advantage enjoyed by the ruthless diplomacy of the Nazis; and an important chance to make use of it was almost at once to appear.

The last embers of the burned houses of Addis Ababa had scarcely died out, Mr. Eden at Geneva had barely "liquidated" the League's disastrous intervention in the Ethiopian War and the echoes of Haile Selassie's last, warning appeal had hardly disappeared from the newspapers when the world was suddenly shocked by still a new war crisis, coming from a direction of which no one had been thinking. On July 17, 1936, a civil war broke out against the republican government of Spain. Spain, shut off in the far corner of Europe and no such vital part of the European system as were Austria and Czechoslovakia, might seem to have little to do with the problems of Berlin, Paris, London, Rome and Moscow. But the powers were to have a great deal to do with Spain; and this civil war, like the war in distant Ethiopia, was to have far-reaching effects on Europe.

The Spaniards had deposed their king five years before and set up a liberal republican government.

But they had not done away with the deep conflicts between the old and the new within their own country—between the democratic, the liberal and the radical groups on the one hand and the great conservative interests of the big landowners, the army and the church on the other—nor with the more and more bitter divisions in men's minds between Fascism and Communism and democracy which were rising through the world, and were to help make those conflicts more and more insoluble. When the liberals were in power they pressed sweeping reforms which angered the conservatives; when the conservatives came to power and began to undo the reforms, there was a bloody rebellion by the Left * which was put down with great cruelty. Finally in the spring of 1936 another election brought a "united front" government of liberal and radical parties back into office.

This was anything but a Communist government. Most of its members were actually very moderate middle-class democrats, and the small Spanish Communist party had few representatives in Parliament and little influence at the beginning. The native radical groups, however, were more important; it was hard to keep all the restless elements of the people in control; there was a good deal of violence that spring and a series of political gang murders. For these the conservatives and the radicals seem to have been about equally responsible. But the conservatives fiercely denounced the new government as noth-

* See page 123.

ing but a collection of "Reds" and revolutionaries incapable of keeping order; and the high officers of the army began to plot a sudden military uprising which would "save Spain," as they said, by sweeping away the republic and replacing it with some sort of dictatorship on the Fascist or Nazi model.

In mid-July the plot was sprung. General Francisco Franco, whom the government had exiled to the Canary Islands because they suspected him, was flown secretly to Spanish Morocco, where he raised the garrison in revolt and seized the colony. In Madrid and the other chief cities the officers called upon their troops to mutiny, and a day or two later Franco flew to the mainland to take command. But by that time the first blow had already failed. The government hastily called out the workers and armed them as a militia; with these, and what loyal troops and officers they could find, they surrounded and suppressed the Madrid garrison, thus saving the capital; Barcelona and other chief cities were saved in the same way; and the rebellious soldiers got a firm hold only over Spanish Morocco, the area in the southwest around Cadiz and Seville, and an area around Burgos in the north. The uprising had miscarried. It had, however, left the conservative rebellion with strong bases from which it was to wage what turned out to be nearly a three years' civil war. But it was not the Spanish conservatives and military alone who were thus to "save Spain" over the ruins of three years of frightful savagery, destruction and bitterness. Even from the beginning it was not purely a civil war. For, even before the actual outbreak, both Hitler and Mussolini had already decided to lend it their aid.

Germany had taken no part in the League sanctions against Italy, and since the Ethiopian War the two dictators had been drawing much more closely together. Both of them now found reasons for crushing democratic government in Spain and helping to establish there a Fascist dictatorship. Each made much of his character as a defender of Europe from the "Reds"; the Spanish Republic was not particularly Red, but could be made to look like it, and its destruction would be a spectacular triumph adding to the dictators' prestige at home and abroad. It would also serve as a cover for attaining more practical ends. A dictatorship in Spain sympathetic to Italy and Germany would immensely weaken the democracies. It would threaten Great Britain's hold on Gibraltar and therefore on Italy's Mediterranean lifeline—a hold which the Italians deeply resented. It would create a new danger for France. Already confronted by a rearming Germany on their eastern frontier, the French would have to face a possibly hostile power along their southern frontier as well. In war Spain might be turned into an air and submarine base for Italy or Germany from which the two democracies or their vital lines of communication could be menaced.

Both the dictators had had their agents in Spain

and their contacts with those organizing the rebellion. On the day it broke out a whole squadron of military airplanes was flown from Italy to Spanish Morocco to lend aid. Three squadrons of German military aviation and an anti-aircraft battery were in Spain either before the rebellion began or almost immediately afterward; and the Germans have declared that before the end of July, German and Italian pilots had won command of the air from the Spanish air force, a large part of which had remained loyal to the government. From that time on the two dictators poured airplanes, tanks, anti-aircraft and anti-tank artillery and tens of thousands of organized "volunteer" troops into Spain. With few weapons, with few trustworthy professional officers or trained men, with little beside the fierce but inexperienced and often undisciplined devotion of the Spanish workers and small farmers, the Spanish Republic was desperately fighting for its life against perhaps a third of its own people, against the Moorish mercenaries that Franco ferried over from Morocco, against Fascist Italy and against Hitler's Germany.

The French and British democracies were by no means blind to what it would mean to them if dictatorship should crush still another hopeful experiment in democracy, and if Italy and Germany should establish their power on the Spanish peninsula. And there was even more reason for alarm because they could see Hitler and Mussolini coming steadily nearer to what looked like a real alliance. There had been a

clear warning of this in the first days of July, just
before the beginning of the Spanish war; and it was
a warning which concerned the most delicate and
most dangerous spot in Europe. Chancellor Schuschnigg of Austria had made an agreement with Adolf
Hitler.

To understand what this meant you must remember how Austria served as the keystone of the whole
European arch.* You must remember that Mussolini's
dislike of the idea of a German annexation of Austria, which would bring German troops to his own
northern frontier, was one of the main things that
kept him apart from Hitler.† You must remember
that it was Mussolini who had been propping up the
Austrian government in its struggles against the Austrian Nazis and their German backers.‡ Now Germany and Austria had come to an agreement. Hitler
solemnly promised to recognize Austria's independence; he declared that the Austrian Nazis were Austria's own domestic affair, in which he would not
interfere either "directly or indirectly"; but in return Austria declared herself a "German state"—
whatever that might mean—and Schuschnigg took
two representatives of the pro-Nazi opinion into his
cabinet as a sign that peace had been made.

It was a pretty dangerous kind of peace. In return
for Hitler's promise to leave Austria alone, Schuschnigg had brought the Nazis into a position from

* See page 79.   ‡ See page 122.
† See page 115.

which they would be much better able to wreck his government in case Hitler should decide that the promise was not worth keeping. But Mussolini sent his congratulations. That meant either that the Italian dictator trusted the promise, or, if he did not, that he was willing to let Austria go. In either case, Austria was no longer a question to divide Mussolini from Hitler; and as the two now began quite actively (though secretly) to co-operate in their support of the rebellious Spanish generals, anxious politicians in Paris and London could already see the outlines of a great dictatorial alliance whose power would reach right across Europe from East Prussia on the Baltic to Cadiz on the Atlantic.

What were they to do about it? As had happened so many times before, they did not know. Through August and September the rebel armies were consolidating their positions, joining hands with each other and pushing their columns rapidly toward Madrid, wiping out government supporters on their way with a savagery often incredible. The government was desperately trying to arm, organize and train the workers and was appealing for help wherever it could be had. France and Great Britain might have shipped into it the arms and volunteers to match the dictators' contributions to General Franco. But in France and particularly in Great Britain there were many conservatives who sympathized with Franco rather than with the "Red" government of the republic. In the first weeks nobody in the democracies knew the real extent of Italian and German aid; nobody could be sure that if Franco won he really would be a puppet of the dictators; as his armies pushed onward across the dry Spanish plateau country it looked as though he would soon win anyway and that it would therefore be wiser to try to keep his friendship than to fight him. And that was not all. While the democracies hesitated, the Communists were active. Stalin's agents, like those of Hitler and Mussolini, had been at work in Spain before the war. Because they were among the stronger and better disciplined groups available, the government was making use of the Spanish radical and Communist organizations, for it had to make use of anything that would help; and presently it appeared that important assistance was on the way from Soviet Russia itself.

The democracies hesitated still more. All their fears of Communism at home revived. If they began to send in arms and munitions to the Spanish government in order to prevent a Fascist dictatorship they might only end by helping set up a Communist one; and worse than that, they might very well bring on a general European war while they were about it. If the democracies helped the Spanish Republic, the dictators would only double the assistance they were sending to Franco; the democracies would then have to increase their own efforts correspondingly, and soon the great powers would be fighting directly with each other. Clearly the wise, cautious thing to do was to stay out of any such entanglement as that.

The thing to do was to keep the war from "spreading."

Instead of heaping their own munitions on the flames, the democracies should try rather to prevent the others from piling on any more than they had sent already. Instead of going in themselves, even secretly or indirectly, they should try to get the dictators out. The Spaniards should be left to settle their own quarrel in their own way. British and French diplomacy went busily to work collecting pledges from the Germans, the Italians and the Russians that all would avoid lending help in the war; and in September the famous "Non-Intervention Committee," with representatives of all these powers, was set up in London to see that the pledges were fulfilled. The only result was that the democracies kept the pledges and stayed out; the dictator states went cheerfully on pouring in men and munitions, while using the Non-Intervention Committee mainly as a convenient place in which they could heatedly deny all charges that they were doing so.

Franco in the meanwhile was pressing on toward Madrid, his armies powerfully strengthened by Moorish troops, Italian tanks and German aircraft and artillery. He took Toledo in October. In the first days of November his troops were in the villages on the outskirts of Madrid; his bombs and artillery shells were landing in its main streets, outside its sandbagged shops and cafés. The Italian and German diplomats, at the same time, had been busy in their

own way; and on October 25, at Hitler's country
house at Berchtesgaden, high up amid the peace and
loveliness of the Bavarian Alps, there was signed the
agreement between Italy and Germany which the
Austrian accord had seemed to forecast. It was in
form an agreement to combat Communism together.
But it meant that the two dictators had settled their
differences, they had divided Europe into each one's
"sphere of interest," and henceforward they would
stand almost as allies against the world.

Madrid was about to fall. But at the last moment
the government's worker-militia—stiffened by the
celebrated International Brigade formed out of the
liberals, the radicals, the anti-Fascists and anti-Nazis
who had flocked in from all over the world to help
in this fight—rallied grimly behind the wrecks of
Madrid's outer houses. And then on November 17
there roared up over the capital whole organized
squadrons of Soviet airplanes, flown by Soviet pilots,
on their way to engage the Franco aviation. Soviet
Russia was participating as directly in the war as
were Italy and Germany. Madrid was saved, and was
to hold out through all the two years and more of
warfare that were to come. But after this, "non-intervention" became little more than a rather bad joke.

Mussolini began to ship organized divisions of "volunteers" into Spain, until there were anywhere from
40,000 to perhaps 100,000 Italian troops fighting for
Franco; the Nazis used Spain as a testing ground
for their latest airplanes and anti-aircraft and anti-

tank artillery and sent their pilots there for practical training in war. The Russians continued to help the government, but nothing like so powerfully; the French and British sat in the Non-Intervention Committee, twisted their hands, and pretended not to know what was going on. They did not want a war. They did not want to get any more involved with the Russians than they could help. They did not know what to do. The two dictators continued to denounce Communism and to strengthen the understanding between them—the understanding which soon began to be known as the "Rome-Berlin Axis."

8. THE ROME-BERLIN AXIS

FOR ANOTHER YEAR THE ROME-Berlin Axis was in fact the chief axis around which the history of Europe turned. The two dictators did not have to bother with parliaments or public opinion; they knew, or seemed to know, what they wanted, and in Spain and elsewhere they were going about getting it with a cold-blooded "realism"

and a bland contempt for moral pretenses. Mussolini
continued to enlist his Italians by the thousand, telling them they were being sent to police Ethiopia
but landing them instead at Cadiz to serve under
Franco's flag. Franco had been stopped against the
western outskirts of Madrid in November. In March,
1937, some four Italian mechanized divisions were
sent down the long road from the northeast, to take
the capital in the rear. But the weather was wet and
the roads muddy; and they were badly led, without
enough protection against surprise. They had reached
nearly to Guadalajara when the government and
Soviet aviation swept suddenly down to bomb and
machinegun the long columns jammed together
upon the roads or bogged in the muddy ground. The
Italians were caught and slaughtered without being
able to reply—much as their countrymen had slaughtered the unhappy Ethiopians the year before—and
the government infantry came up to turn a defeat
into a rout. Mussolini, however, only put fresh troops
into the country and improved their leadership; and
this rout at Guadalajara was to be the single really
complete victory won by the government in the
whole course of the war.

When, a few weeks later, a government airplane
took the German "pocket battleship" *Deutschland*
by surprise as she was lying in harbor at Mallorca,
and landed a direct bomb hit on the vessel's upper-
works, Hitler responded in a cold fury. A German
naval squadron was ordered to bombard the coast

town of Almería, which had no means of defense, as a "lesson." The shells wrecked a good many houses, killed a good many helpless women and children and so upheld the Nazi honor and prestige. They also made it clear that Hitler would stand no nonsense about having his way in Spain. But would he stop there? In Austria Chancellor Schuschnigg was still struggling against the Nazi agitators and gangsters; their conspiracies for overthrowing the government and bringing about the *Anschluss* of Austria and Germany flourished more than ever in spite of the agreement with Hitler. Or was it because of the agreement?

In Czechoslovakia the Nazi Sudeten-German party of Konrad Henlein had drawn or driven nearly all the Sudeten Germans into its ranks and was now the second largest party in the country. Under its continuous clamor for autonomy the Czech government was getting itself involved in a very dangerous course. On the one hand it was trying to pacify the Sudetens with concessions; on the other hand, their agitation was driving it to a greater strictness in self-defense, and a greater hesitation about giving the Sudetens a freedom which Henlein might use to destroy the state. In consequence, Henlein refused to be satisfied with any concessions which were offered, while the failure to grant more only fed the flames of his agitation. The shadow of Hitler's Germany was already dark over Austria; it was deepening over Czechoslovakia as well.

Mussolini at the same time was using the new strength which the association with Germany gave him. His propaganda was trying to rouse the Arabs of the Near East against Britain. He made a new treaty of friendship with Yugoslavia. In its actual terms, perhaps, it did not say much; but it seemed to end the hostility between the two countries and to mean that France was losing the support of another of the Central European allies on whom she had counted to uphold the post-war system. In 1934 Hitler had made a nonaggression treaty with the Poles, and France could no longer rely on them; if Yugoslavia should now be drawn into the Rome-Berlin Axis, French power would be much further weakened. And Hitler all this time was working his munitions factories night and day, building up his army and beginning the mighty chain of fortifications along his western front which would end the French Army's ability to interfere with whatever he might do in Central Europe.

In the Axis there were, perhaps, the real beginnings of a new European system—or there would have been, if the two dictators could have used their growing strength and solidarity to organize some kind of workable arrangement to which the other great powers might have been able to agree. As it was, all that the Axis seemed to hold out to the others was a threat, and a threat which was worse because it was so vague, because neither dictator ever set any definite limit to his ambitions, because there was nothing to show where this new power might stop. To many in France and Britain matters seemed already reaching the point where the only choice would be between having to fight or making a complete surrender. But the democratic governments could do neither. The savage Spanish fighting dragged on, accustoming the world to fresh horrors and violences and confusing all the issues. Was Europe's basic problem really a struggle between democracy and dictatorship? If so, then Soviet Russia, one of the most extreme of the dictatorships, could not be brought in to fight with the democracies. Or was it a struggle between radicalism and reaction? If so, then all the more conservative forces within the democracies would find themselves much closer to Hitler and Mussolini than to the other side. The democratic governments drifted through a series of half-hearted expedients.

Both France and Britain began at last to go to work on rearming themselves with something to match the modern weapons being hammered out in Germany and Italy. But the British at the same time continued to cling to the hope that they could win Mussolini away from the Axis, re-establish friendly relations with him and either get him out of Spain or make sure that he would keep his promise to get out when the civil war was over. Very little was to come of it. And while the diplomatists were busy with such shifting and more or less useless maneuvers as these in Rome or Berlin or the lesser capitals, the democracies began to find themselves with something new to think about.

Something very strange was happening in Russia. In the summer of 1936 the news had come from Moscow that sixteen men, including Kamenev and Zinoviev—who had for years been two of the most important and best-known leaders of the Bolshevist revolution—were about to be tried on charges of having conspired to assassinate Stalin and other prominent governmental figures. The idea that so grave a conspiracy as this could grow up within the supposedly united ranks of the Bolshevist leadership seemed surprising in itself; but the trial which almost immediately followed was far more surprising still. The accused men did not even try to defend themselves; instead, they took the witness stand in succession, each apparently trying to confess to a blacker guilt than the others. Within a few days they had all been condemned and it was announced that they had been shot.

The world did not know what to make of it. It seemed impossible that these could have been genuine confessions of genuine crimes; on the other hand, it seemed unbelievable that Stalin could have extorted, and then published to the world, false confessions which showed the Soviet Union riddled with such treason as this. Yet this trial was only a beginning. In January, 1937, there was a second sensational trial with more prominent Bolshevists among the defendants—Radek, one of the most celebrated of Bolshevist journalists, Sokolnikov, who had been ambassador to Great Britain, and Piatokov, formerly in the administration of heavy industry. Again there was an amazing series of confessions (which the Moscow authorities took care to broadcast through the world) in which these men accused themselves of having conspired with Japan and with Nazi Germany to encourage them to make war on Russia with the idea of overthrowing Stalin's rule.

Could there be any truth in it? The Japanese, the Germans and everyone else outside Russia whom the confessions had mentioned dismissed the story as pure invention. It seemed fantastic to imagine that these older Bolshevist leaders could actually conspire against their country with Adolf Hitler—whose whole career had been founded upon the unmeasured denunciation of Communism and all its works. Yet for a long time people had been asking themselves whether there was really so much difference between the Nazi dictatorship in Germany and the Communist dictatorship in Russia. Nazi and Communist ideas were really a great deal alike at bottom; if only the Nazis and Communists stopped calling each other names, was there so much to keep them apart?

The idea of Germany and Russia—the one with her great industries, her technical ability, her need for raw materials and markets, and the other with her vast, undeveloped resources and her immense man-power—joining their forces against the rest of the world was an idea much older than Hitler. The two nations had been closely associated in Bismarck's time. Just after the World War Soviet Russia had supported republican Germany against the victor powers; * and it was believed that the high officers of the German Army had kept alive the dream of a Russo-German alliance even while Hitler and his Nazis were talking great plans for wars against Russia. German officers had worked with the Red Army, and it was said that many of the pilots with whom the Nazis had begun secretly to build up their air power had got their training with the Soviet Air Force. Just as the German Army was more friendly to Russia than the Nazis, so the Red Army was supposed to be more friendly to Germany than was Stalin. Could there be any truth in this story of widespread conspiracy against Stalin between the older Bolshevik leaders and the Germans? There were few more dramatic public trials in Moscow. But in the summer of 1937 it was suddenly announced that Marshal Tukhachevsky, the ranking general in the Red Army and the man who was considered the best soldier in Russia, had been secretly tried and shot, along with seven other of the highest Soviet generals. The "purge" was now fully under way.

No one today knows the details of that strange episode; no one knows just what was behind it, or how many died or were exiled in the fanatical hunt after secret enemies and traitors which ran like a poison through the whole Russian community for

* See page 22.

something over two years. Generals and admirals, high government executives, important diplomatic officials simply disappeared—some to Siberia, some before firing squads, some on published charges and some without even an announcement that they had gone. Probably thousands of lesser officials and local figures went with them—no one knows. The French Army, which had been hoping for Russian support, believed that something like one-half the huge Soviet officer corps had been shot or dismissed, and that the Red Army's efficiency had been hopelessly wrecked.

New men appeared in hundreds of important posts. Inexperienced to begin with, they were paralyzed by fear of what had happened to their predecessors. While the "purge" was running its extraordinary course, two things only were clear. Josef Stalin, for whatever reason, was turning his dictatorship into a personal absolutism, more like the half-Oriental tyranny of the Czars than the brave "dictatorship of the proletariat," with its lofty and progressive ideals, for which Communism was supposed to stand. And while he was doing it, Russian influence in Europe was fading away. Soviet intervention in Spain began to dwindle. The democratic governments began to lose whatever confidence they may have had in the efficiency of Russia as a military ally; while many of the liberal groups in the Western countries who had believed in the "united front" against Fascism began to lose confidence in the purposes of a government which could use methods so shocking and so reactionary as these purges and treason trials. The idea of a strong British-French-Russian combination to hold the new Germany in check—an idea with which the democratic diplomatists had played, at least, ever since Russia's entry into the League in 1934—lost its force as the Russians turned their principal energies to the business of denouncing and shooting their own leaders. The democracies were correspondingly weakened; their policies were contradictory and their leading men irresolute. The Rome-Berlin Axis seemed only stronger than ever.

And the world seemed sinking only deeper than ever into violence and bloodshed. The Spanish War went on and on, with no end in sight for its horrors and suffering. And in July, 1937, the Japanese—who had entered into a vague sort of alliance with Hitler's Germany—resumed their war on China. There was a mysterious "incident" on the dusty plain outside Peking, in which a column of Japanese troops supposedly on maneuvers got into a battle with Chinese forces. Three years later the Japanese were still calling their struggle in China an "incident"; but it had quickly broadened into a vast war of conquest, for which once more there seemed to be no end, with no limit to the brutal agonies which it inflicted.

Through motion pictures, through news photographs and despatches, the world could follow almost step by step the wrecking of the great cities of Shanghai and Nanking by merciless air bombing and by the trampling armies; it could not so easily see all the

death and suffering and starvation and disease which
were spread through the hundreds of millions of Chinese people as the Japanese columns fought their
way deeper and deeper into the country. But everywhere people were still further accustomed to the
idea of war and violence as natural and unavoidable
in these strange new times. Everywhere the wheels
of the munitions factories turned faster; the armies
and navies and air forces grew larger and more threatening, men more and more often asked themselves,
not whether a new great war was coming, but only
when and how it would come.

It did not even seem so very surprising when ships
carrying supplies to Spanish government ports began
to be torpedoed without warning in the Mediterranean by mysterious submarines. General Franco
had only a couple of submarines under his flag so far
as anyone knew, and they could not possibly be doing all the damage. It seemed very probable that
Italian submarines were quietly lending him their assistance. It once would have been almost unbelievable
that a great power could secretly send out its own
warships to destroy vessels belonging to countries
with which it was at peace. It was not so difficult
to believe it now; but this appearance of what
amounted to piracy was still extraordinary enough
to drive Britain and France to action. In September,
1937, they summoned a conference of the powers
to deal with these unknown "pirate" submarines.
Italy and Germany refused to attend. The British

and French held the conference anyway, and together with Russia and six of the smaller Mediterranean countries they signed what is known as the Nyon Agreement. They would patrol the Mediterranean with their own naval forces, and attack and destroy any "pirate" submarines they might catch operating against shipping. For once the great democracies had taken a strong stand; and it was remarkable that the activities of these unknown submarines ceased immediately.

It was an example of "collective security"—the principle, which the League of Nations had been established to make effective, of all joining together to put down a threat or an aggression by anyone. And it had succeeded. But it was a pretty small example, after all—and it was also the last. Some argued that the League might be brought back to real life again, and that if only the great democracies were firm enough, the dictators would always back down. But nothing came of it. In this same month Mussolini paid a grand visit to Hitler in Berlin. There were several days of speech-making, of tremendous military spectacles in which the new German Army and air force, with all the new weapons they had forged, were displayed to the Italian; there were innumerable photographs of the two dictators greeting each other, standing together in reviewing stands, at state dinners, making plain to all the solidity and might of the Rome-Berlin Axis. The Nyon Agreement had worked; but it was soon forgotten. In December,

Mussolini scornfully announced Italy's formal withdrawal from the League.

So the year 1937 ran out. No new European system had been put together; the national building blocks were more than ever like loaded bombs. In Spain at Christmas time there was bitter fighting in the cruel snows around Teruel. There was a vast misery in China. The Nazis were rapidly turning Germany into one huge machine for making war, with the people drilled and regimented in every side of their lives, with the secret police everywhere and the concentration camps filling up, with every book and newspaper and radio broadcast censored into an instrument of propaganda. Already thousands of German Jews were wandering through Europe and America, driven out of their homes by a cold-blooded and barbaric persecution. Many of the finest German writers and artists, doctors and teachers, had been exiled and their works prohibited in Germany because they were Jews. In Austria, a government which had destroyed the workers' organizations that might perhaps have protected it was watching Nazi agitation threatening to destroy it in turn, and was helpless to stop the trend. The same kind of thing was threatening to split Czechoslovakia in two. In Rumania a Nazi-Fascist organization called the Iron Guard was beating up Jews, agitating in the streets and threatening the government of King Carol, and it helped bring a pro-German, anti-Semitic prime minister to power. The Poles, who had signed nonaggression treaties with both Germany and Russia, were trying desperately to be neutral and were hoping for the best.

"The situation in Central Europe," as a correspondent in Vienna has described it, "now began to resemble a scene in some crook play where someone has shot out the lights and the other actors, revolvers in hand, listen intently for a sign of movement to know in what direction they should prepare to shoot." There were "diplomatic jitters" in all directions. The Russians were still busy with their purge. The French were getting a start, but rather a tardy one, on the modernization of their armaments; the British, getting an even slower start, were hoping that they would be let alone and that somehow things would still turn out all right. The whole air of Europe seemed poisoned by savagery and gangsterism, by violent policies and barbaric teachings. Men more and more were coming to feel that this could not last; that sooner or later there was bound to be an explosion somewhere. But as yet nothing definite or final had happened.

In 1933, in 1935 and in 1936 Hitler had shocked and shaken Europe by a sudden and violent move * against the established situation. But 1937 had passed, and there had been nothing of quite the same sort. While he was building up his armies, he was still talking peace. Might he not mean it? Perhaps this was not just a pause; perhaps, now that he had freed

* See pages 105, 129, and 145.

Germany of all the principal restrictions laid upon her, he was ready to work more "reasonably" with the others. A group of influential political people in England convinced themselves that there was a good hope of this; they believed the thing to do was to try to work with Hitler instead of against him; and Lord Halifax, a prominent British statesman who was also a devout Christian and a believer in peace, paid an "unofficial" visit to Germany. He stayed with General Goering and talked with Hitler. No one could quite believe that the German dictator really meant to follow the extravagant policies about which he and his Nazi propagandists so often talked. It seemed clear that nobody, least of all the dictators, really wanted a war. Perhaps this pause would last, and everything really would turn out all right.

But then Hitler resumed his march.

PART THREE

THE COMING OF WAR

9. THE KEYSTONE FALLS

FIELD MARSHAL WERNER VON BLOM-berg, the Nazi Minister of War and one of the three or four highest officers of the German Army, was a widower. He was also a handsome, ruddy-faced man with a soldierly figure; and he had an attractive young secretary. The result was quite natural. He fell in love with her. In a saner, more ordinary world this very personal matter in the life of an elderly general could hardly appear as one of the causes of a great war; and indeed, it is not easy to say just how much it really had to do with what followed. But in the fantastic situation at which Europe had arrived by the first days of 1938 there was very little that was either sane or ordinary; and it is a fact that this romance of von Blomberg and his blue-eyed secre-tary was the starting-point, at least, for a whole train of tremendous events that were now to come with breathless speed.

They were married privately on January 12 by a Berlin magistrate, but with two very distinguished witnesses—Adolf Hitler himself and Colonel General

Goering—and they set out on a leisurely honeymoon trip to the lovely island of Capri. It was only when they stopped off on the way to stroll through the streets of Leipzig that the bride's name became public. According to the police records she was a person of allegedly doubtful character and of a social station so humble as to outrage the very strict ideas on such matters which had always been held by the officer corps of the German Army. The Field Marshal and his bride went on to Capri. But behind them the newspapers of the world began to buzz with rumors of another great political crisis under way in the secret inner circles of Hitler's régime.

As usual, no one knows exactly what happened. Apparently the high Army officers, most of whom had never been too sympathetic toward Hitler and his Nazis anyway, rose in a kind of rebellion against the indignity which they felt the Nazi War Minister had done to them. Apparently Hitler was furious with von Blomberg for having got him to approve the marriage by his attendance. Apparently he was also furious with the Army High Command. But, more than that, it would seem that his anger over the whole affair served as the emotional trigger which finally touched off, in the mind of this always sudden and emotional politician, vastly larger plans which he had been considering and preparing, at the same time that it gave him a good opportunity to set them in operation. On February 4, the world learned that the rumors of a crisis had been correct.

There had been a second German "purge"—though this time only by dismissals and not by bloodshed. Field Marshal von Blomberg was no longer Minister of War, and it seemed likely that he and his new wife would be staying for a long time in Capri. General von Fritsch, the commander-in-chief of the Army, considered one of the best soldiers in Germany and also a leading representative of the High Command's distrust of the Nazis, was dismissed; along with him went twelve other high Army and air force generals. They were replaced by less imposing officers, more subservient to the Nazis, while Hitler himself took over the post of Minister of War. Nor did the changes stop there. Schacht, the brilliant and tricky but on the whole conservative Minister of Economics, was replaced by a Nazi figurehead; while von Neurath, the conservative Minister of Foreign Affairs, was removed and his position given to Joachim von Ribbentrop—a reckless and adventurous product of the Nazi era, whose "expert" advice to his leader was to have much to do with the next two years of world history.

Once more Hitler, in a sudden move, had swept away possible domestic opposition to his plans. He had got rid of the sound financiers and conservative diplomats who were inclined to insist that there had to be a limit somewhere to what he might risk. He had got rid of the cautious generals who as a rule had opposed his schemes as too bold and dangerous. More than ever he had taken absolute power and

authority into his own hands. The world was not to
wait long before learning how he intended to use
them.

On February 8, just four days after this purge had
taken place, Chancellor Schuschnigg of Austria received a most pressing invitation to visit Chancellor
Hitler in his mountain house at Berchtesgaden. It was
not an invitation to be taken lightly. A year and a
half before the Austrian Chancellor had signed an
agreement with the Nazi leader * under which Hitler
had undertaken to respect Austria's independence;
and it had been proving a very dangerous bargain. It
had not ended the secret and illegal agitation of the
Austrian Nazis. It had not ended the encouragement
and advice they had been getting from Germany. It
had not prevented the treacherous spread of Nazism
through the Austrian police and among government
officials. It had not prevented some, even, of Schuschnigg's own associates in the government, men whom
he trusted, from going over secretly to the Nazi side.
And it had not ended the rumors of a new putsch
which would overthrow the Schuschnigg government and accomplish at last the *Anschluss* of Austria
with Nazi Germany. A "Committee of Seven" had
been set up at the time of the agreement, supposedly
to help in the reconciliation of the Austrian Nazis
and the government; actually, it had turned into
nothing more than a headquarters for the continued
illegal agitation for *Anschluss*. Only two or three

* See page 165.

weeks before the police had at last raided the offices of this committee, and they had found, among other things, a complete plan for a Nazi putsch, under which the little country would first be reduced to turmoil; the German Army would then march in on the pretext of "restoring order." And the plan had borne the initials, not of any Austrian Nazi, but of Rudolf Hess, Adolf Hitler's closest and probably most trusted lieutenant.

It was with this plan before him that Chancellor Schuschnigg listened while not only the German Ambassador but even his own Foreign Secretary urged him to take the road to Berchtesgaden. The Chancellor was well aware of its dangers. Already a story had reached Vienna that Hitler was saying openly that he would "soon have Schuschnigg's head." To accept this invitation and so put himself in Hitler's hands might mean the end of Austria. The others tried to reassure him; Hitler, they argued, only wished to confirm the 1936 agreement. Here was too good a chance to lose to get Hitler's absolutely binding personal promise not to destroy Austrian independence; it would never do to anger him by refusing to go. And, indeed, Chancellor Schuschnigg himself knew that to refuse the invitation might only exasperate the Nazi Führer and so bring on just such a putsch as the Germans had already planned.

Schuschnigg sounded out the Italians; but Mussolini, who in 1934 had moved troops up to the frontier to protect Austria from the Nazis, was now a part-

ner of the Axis and offered no help. The Chancellor
sounded out the French and British; but the great
democracies, though they knew that Austria was the
keystone of the whole European system which they
were trying to maintain, seemed to think the matter
of no importance. Schuschnigg was left standing
alone, and he was helpless. He accepted the invitation. The visit was kept a secret. But before he left
the Chancellor called in one of his most trusted officials, explained where he was going and said that if
he should not come back the other was at once to take
over the Chancellorship.

On the morning of Saturday, February 12, a
motorcar carried the Austrian Chancellor over the
border into Germany; at the frontier he had let the
local police chief into the secret and given orders that
in case he was not back by nine o'clock that evening
the border was to be closed. It was more like a ro-
mantic melodrama than the sober business of states-
manship; but the thing was deadly serious, for all
that. Such was the extraordinary state to which European politics had come. The Chancellor's car rolled
on through the Alpine spurs, in warm and almost
springlike weather. Everywhere the sinister, black-
uniformed SS guards were watching over the road;
everywhere the Chancellor saw German Army troops
coming and going on "maneuvers" which could be
turned at a word into an invasion of Austria. It was
just four years since that other February 12 when
Dollfuss had sent his soldiers and Heimwehr men

against the Socialist workers of Vienna, and so destroyed the last chance for uniting the whole Austrian people in defense of their little republic.* Chancellor Schuschnigg's car swept him up to Hitler's mountain cottage at Berchtesgaden, where the Nazi dictator had so often liked to sit, looking out over the lovely scenery of his native Austria.

There are many stories of what followed. Hitler, it is said, worked himself up into a fury—as he often seemed deliberately to do—screamed and shouted at the Austrian, insulted him, refused to allow him to smoke, accused him of oppressing and starving "my German people in Austria," and finally flung down before him a series of demands. But before being allowed to study them, Schuschnigg was introduced to a high German general who took him into another room and carefully explained the plans already prepared for the invasion of Austria. Then there was a formal luncheon, at a table full of Nazi diplomats and army officers, and the argument was resumed in the afternoon. Hitler's most important demands were, apparently, that the Austrian Nazis who had been jailed for their illegal agitation should be set free, that the Nazis should be taken into Schuschnigg's own party, and, above all, that a Nazi sympathizer should be appointed to the vital post of Minister of the Interior, where he would have control over the police.

To accept these meant surrendering the last chance of defending Austrian independence. Schuschnigg

* See page 112.

tried to resist, but what could he do? He knew he
could count on no support from abroad and little
enough from his own deeply divided people. In return, it is said, for Hitler's promise that he would
publicly repeat his undertaking not to annex the
country—a promise that was never fulfilled—Schuschnigg yielded. It was late when he finally took the road
back down the mountain; and when he reached the
frontier, long after nine o'clock, he found that it had
been closed as he had ordered. He had not, after all,
been murdered, as he evidently thought might happen. But Austria was about to be.

For two or three days more the Austrian government tried to hold out. The Germans held more
"maneuvers" and threatened an immediate invasion
if Hitler's demands were not accepted. Schuschnigg
telephoned Mussolini for help—and was told that the
Italian dictator was away on a skiing trip and could
not be reached. The news of the trip to Berchtesgaden was getting about by this time; there were
many Austrians who felt angrily that they were about
to be "sold to Hitler," but Schuschnigg and his government did not dare to try to rouse the country. It
was better to submit quietly and hope for the best
than to make a fight which it would have been impossible to win. Early on the morning of Wednesday,
February 16, the cabinet was made over. Seyss-Inquart, a Nazi sympathizer whom, however, Schuschnigg still thought to be his friend, was made Minister
of the Interior and the policing of the country placed

in his hands. His first act was to fly to Berlin to get his orders from Adolf Hitler.

There was nervousness, fear and excitement in Vienna; and the newspaper correspondents found a picturesque phrase for the new Minister of the Interior. He was the "Trojan horse"—the cover behind which, as in the old Greek legend, the Nazis had been brought into the heart of the Austrian citadel. But abroad nobody cared very much. The British were full of plans for coming to an agreement with both Hitler and Mussolini; their officials thought that Schuschnigg had acted wisely, and felt relieved that perhaps the Austrian question had really been settled at last without the riots or the invasions which might have forced them to do something about it. On the Sunday, February 20, Hitler was to make a formal speech before his Reichstag which would be broadcast throughout the world. The evening before an anxious group had called on Chancellor Schuschnigg. They were leading Austrian Jews and they had come to ask what they might have to fear. The Chancellor told them "that they and other Jews could face the future with complete confidence." The same evening Seyss-Inquart was back from Berlin. He called in the foreign correspondents. "I wish you would say to the whole world," he told them, "that I am no Trojan horse. I believe that Austria must be an independent, Christian Austria—nothing else but that. No further changes are foreseen now."

Next day came Hitler's speech, shouting and

rumbling and roaring through the radios all round the earth. It was long and rambling, and carefully vague, like most of Hitler's speeches, at the critical places. But it was violent and aggressive; he was, he said, the ruler of 66,000,000 Germans and he left no doubt that he intended to use their armed power as he pleased. There was no pledge of Austrian independence. There was nothing which would have made the Austrian Nazis behave themselves and work with the Schuschnigg government. There was, instead, an ominous passage. In two countries bordering on Germany, Hitler declared, there were "10,000,000 Germans," and it was "intolerable" that they should be oppressed, be made to suffer and be denied the right of "self-determination simply because they are Germans." One country, of course, was Austria, with its 7,000,000 people. The other was Czechoslovakia, with its 3,500,000 Sudetens.

That evening there was a sensation in London, when it was announced that Mr. Anthony Eden, the young Foreign Secretary who had taken office as a supporter of the League and an opponent of both Italian and German fascism, had resigned. It seemed to show that the British government was resolved to let the dictators have their way whatever they did; and that in its desire for peace with them it would even dismiss a Cabinet Minister whom they did not like. The British were disturbed. But in Vienna and the smaller Austrian towns that same night, there was more than disturbance. As if Hitler's speech had been a signal, the illegal Austrian Nazi storm-troop organizations were out; the illegal Nazi battle-cry— "Sieg Heil! Sieg Heil!! Sieg Heil!!! Heil Hitler!"— was roaring through the streets, while the police, now under Seyss-Inquart's command, were bustling about very carefully doing nothing. It was the beginning of the end; and the end was to come quickly.

Two or three days later Schuschnigg, in a speech of his own, made a brave reply. "We have gone to the very limit of concessions, where we must call a halt and say: 'Thus far, but no farther.'" But it was already too late. Over the next couple of week-ends the Nazis devoted themselves to organizing great demonstrations in the provincial towns; and Seyss-Inquart, hurrying about under pretense of keeping order and reconciling the Nazis to the government, actually only inflamed their enthusiasm and urged them on to the moment when a Nazi putsch would make an end of independent Austria. Schuschnigg turned, in these last moments, to the Viennese workers, whose organizations he had helped to crush and make illegal four years before. Now his government was in desperate need of them if it was to live. The Nazis at this time probably had no more than one-third of the Austrian people behind them; but the middle-class and Catholic supporters of Schuschnigg probably numbered only another third, perhaps only a quarter. The rest were the democratic, Socialist or radical followers of the old working-class parties. If Schuschnigg could now bring them to his side in defense of Austria, he would have a commanding majority and the state might yet be saved. The negotiations with the workers' leaders seemed to make progress, and the Chancellor decided to play his last card. In a radio address on Wednesday, March 9, he announced that on the following Sunday the Austrian people would be called upon to vote on the question of whether they wished to retain their independence or to join Nazi Germany.

For years the Austrian Nazis had been clamoring for just such a plebiscite in order to demonstrate their real strength. Now, if Schuschnigg carried the workers with him, it would only reveal their real weakness. From Germany, the Nazi press and radio shrieked and screamed that Schuschnigg was calling up a "Communist mob," that a "Bolshevist revolution" was under way, that Austria had to be "saved" from Communism. Would Hitler allow the plebiscite to take place? In Paris, on Thursday morning, as luck would have it, there was a cabinet crisis over another matter and the French government resigned. It was to take three days before another one could be formed, which meant that through all of Thursday, Friday and Saturday France—the strongest supporter of Austrian independence, the nation which in 1931 had even helped pull down the European economic structure in order to prevent *Anschluss* *—was without a government and helpless. It was the kind of opportunity which Hitler knew how to seize. At ten

* See page 84.

o'clock on Friday morning—with the Chancellor's
campaign for the plebiscite well under way, with
Schuschnigg's supporters parading and cheering in
the streets and the loudspeakers shouting their propaganda to vote for a free Austria—the Chancellor received an ultimatum from Berlin, handed to him by
the pro-Nazis he had taken into his Cabinet. There
must be no plebiscite.

The Chancellor issued orders to begin the mobilization of the Austrian Army. The answer was a second ultimatum. About three o'clock in the afternoon,
Schuschnigg gave way—there was nothing else he
could do—and agreed to cancel the plans for the vote
on Sunday. It was not enough. Within an hour still
another ultimatum arrived direct from Berlin:
Schuschnigg himself must resign and a government
named by Hitler must be set up in Austria. If he had
not done so by 7:30 that evening, a German army
of 200,000 men, already massed upon the border,
would march. About seven, listeners to the Vienna
radio heard an announcer break into the gay music
which had been playing: "In a few moments you will
hear an important announcement." There was a silence, and then the voice of Schuschnigg: "This day
has confronted us with a tragic and decisive situation. . . ." Briefly and solemnly he described the
ultimatum which had been received; the German
propaganda stories of disorder in the country were,
he said, "lies from A to Z"; he had yielded only to
force:

> Since we were not prepared, even in this ter-
> rible situation, to shed blood, we decided to
> order the troops to offer no resistance. . . .
> And so I take leave of the Austrian people with
> a German word of farewell uttered from the
> depths of my heart: "God protect Austria."

With dignity he walked for the last time down the
front steps of his Chancellery. The Nazi storm
troops, armed now and with their swastika badges
in plain sight, were swarming into the streets, taking
over important buildings, hunting out Schuschnigg's
followers or joining the mobs already shouting after
the Jews and Catholics or "heiling" Hitler and Seyss-
Inquart. A car was waiting to rush the ex-Chancellor
to the airport, where a plane was ready to carry him
to safety. He refused; his place, he said, was with
Austria, and he ordered the driver to take him home.
He was put under arrest there that night; and he has
been held prisoner, without trial, from that moment
until this.

Sometime during the night Seyss-Inquart was
named Chancellor; his first act was to "appeal" to
Berlin to send troops to "restore order." Whether
they were already on the way or not makes little difference. By morning—Saturday, March 12—the German columns were streaming down the roads from
the frontier and the German air-force planes were
roaring over Vienna; before the day was over German advance detachments had reached right across
the country and were shaking hands with Musso-

lini's border guards on the Italian frontier. Seyss-Inquart had told the correspondents just three weeks before that he was no "Trojan horse"; now the Trojan horse had perfectly fulfilled his function, and his sham "independent" government did not last two days. By noon on Saturday Heinrich Himmler, the dreaded chief of the Nazi SS guards and secret police, had reached the Chancellery in Vienna; and at four o'clock in the afternoon Adolf Hitler himself, with a long line of motorcars, rolled across the border and into Braunau, his birthplace. Through frenzied crowds of Austrian Nazis, cheering wildly and throwing flowers before him on the roadway, he went on to stay the night at Linz.

It was exactly one month since Chancellor Schuschnigg had gone to lunch with Hitler at Berchtesgaden. It was exactly three weeks since he had told the group of Jews who called on him that they had nothing to fear. Schuschnigg himself was now under arrest; during Friday night hundreds upon hundreds, not only of Jews but of Catholics, Communists, liberal leaders, important men in the Schuschnigg government, had been jamming the railway stations and airports, packing the trains and blocking the highways with their motorcars in a frantic rush to escape the Nazi terror. These people were not fleeing from Austria merely because they disliked dictatorship or disagreed with Hitler. They were fleeing, most of them, for their lives.

Few got away, so quickly did it all happen. The

trains were stopped; the roads were guarded; the
airports were watched. Men and women of all sorts,
Jews and non-Jews, were seized by the storm troopers, beaten, robbed, shot, or, what was often worse,
thrown into concentration camps. For weeks these
brutalities—for which the Austrian Nazis seem to
have been mainly responsible—were to go on, chiefly
against the Jews, but against Catholics and Communists and liberals as well. Jews were deprived of their
businesses, their shops raided or destroyed; they were
plundered of their money, even their furniture; they
were flung out of their jobs, allowed no chance of
escaping the country and no way of making a living
while they stayed in it. When they were expelled,
other countries would not take them in, and one
wretched colony of Jews lived for months in shacks
on a little sand-bank in the Danube between Austria
and Czechoslovakia. In Vienna Jews were insulted
and tormented in every way imaginable; they were
made to scrub sidewalks, being forced to dip their
bare hands in the pails of acid cleaning fluid while
they did so, or put to any other sort of useless and
degrading work the storm troopers could invent.
Hundreds killed themselves as the only way of escape; probably many more, both Jews and non-Jews,
who were listed as having done so had in reality been
shot by the Nazis. And there were countless others,
including many of the chief men in Austria, who
simply vanished without trace into the terrors of the
concentration camps.

The rest of the world looked on appalled—but what could anyone do? On the Saturday when Hitler reached Linz, the French were still trying to form a government. There was a story that in London Lord Halifax, who had succeeded Mr. Eden as Foreign Minister, paced his big office room that afternoon exclaiming: "Horrible! Horrible! I never thought they would do it." But they had done it. In Vienna on Sunday evening the foreign correspondents were called in to the government press bureau and told that by a new law just signed by Seyss-Inquart, Austria had become a province of Germany. There would be a plebiscite later on in which the Austrian people would have a chance to vote their "confirmation" of this decree. But a vote now could have only one result. On Monday, Hitler himself at last came on to Vienna, to address the enormous and frantically cheering Nazi crowds and to review the columns of German infantry and artillery and tanks that he had brought with him. Then he flew back to Germany. Austria was dead. Vienna, which had been for centuries one of the great imperial capitals of Europe, was now only a German provincial city, conquered by the obscure postcard painter who had once starved in her streets, dreaming his bitter and fantastic political dreams.

Austria was dead. The keystone had fallen from the European arch. The World War peace treaties, of course, had been torn up long before; the League of Nations was powerless; the post-war system had

reached final collapse with the invasion of the Rhineland two years earlier. But up to this moment the
territorial settlements made in 1919 had, for the most
part, survived. Now Adolf Hitler, with his strange
combination of adroitness, skill and brute force, had
torn even those to shreds. There was another joke
going round in London at the height of the crisis.
"That noise you hear is the sound of the blinders falling from the eyes of the British Conservative leaders."
And a news despatch on March 12 reported that "the
British Government began seriously and anxiously
today to consider what it would do if the German
mailed fist descended soon upon Czechoslovakia."

What would they do? In Spain in these same days
General Franco, with his German and Italian allies,
was opening a great campaign which was in a few
weeks to cut the government armies in two and was
to prove in the end to have been the decisive campaign of the war. Hitler had made his triumphant
entry into Vienna on Monday. On Wednesday,
Thursday and Friday of the same week the great and
crowded city of Barcelona was subjected to an inten-
sive, methodical air bombing by Italian aviation from
Mallorca—four to five raids every day, at irregular
times, with the latest and deadliest bombs known.
These frightful missiles crashed and roared in the
streets, sweeping the helpless crowds, killing and
wounding men, women and children, and shattering
the nerves of those who were not hurt. It was like
a demonstration of what a great modern war might

do to the finest capitals of Europe, and it was a horrible one. With the bombs there also came down leaflets. "Surrender," they said, "or die." Was that really the message which the dictator governments had brought to Europe? If so, there were many free men, some thought, who might have to die.

10. DEALING WITH DICTATORS

AUSTRIA WAS GONE; AND OF THE "10,000,000 Germans" beyond his borders of whom Hitler had spoken on February 20, some 7,000,000 were now under his swastika flag. The French and British only threw up their hands and accepted the situation. There were no conferences, protests, appeals to the League, as there had been after Hitler's earlier strokes. What was the use? And after all, Austria really had been a German state; a great many Austrians, at least, had passionately desired union with Hitler's Germany; the change was not so unreasonable, and it would be folly to send young Frenchmen and Englishmen to die in battle merely

to keep these two kindred peoples apart. But how
about those other 3,500,000 million "Germans" living
in Czechoslovakia? There was a very different problem.

The Sudeten Germans of Czechoslovakia were
only a minority, though an important minority, in
the country where they lived. They could not be
"brought home to Germany," as the Nazi propagandists were fond of putting it, without shattering
one of the most prosperous, the most enlightened
and the most genuinely democratic of the nations
which had been set up by the peace of 1919. If,
after having taken Austria, Hitler should go on to
seize the Sudeten areas of Czechoslovakia, it would
break up the country's economy—separate its farms
from its factories, cut its road and railway systems
to pieces—dislocate its life and do even worse than
that. The Sudetens lived all around the borders of
Czechoslovakia, on the slopes of the semicircular
mountain chain by which the country was protected.
If you look at the map you will see how those mountains stood like a wall or bastion, defending not only
Czechoslovakia itself from the Germans, but defending the whole Danube Valley, the whole of Southeastern and Eastern Europe. In them, the Czechs had
built the strong chain of modern fortifications—a
"little Maginot Line," as it was called—on which
their safety rested. But it was just in this vital mountain area that the German-speaking Sudetens were
most thickly concentrated. If they should "go home

to Germany" (to which they had never belonged) they would take with them Czechoslovakia's one chance of self-defense. They would take with them the fortress gate to Southeastern and Eastern Europe, and deliver it into Hitler's hands. With Austria fallen, was Czechoslovakia to come next?

On the night of March 11-12, while the German columns were rumbling up to the Austrian frontier, the German Minister in Prague had telephoned the Czech foreign office more than once to make sure that the Czech Army was not mobilizing. No doubt it was comforting to the Czechs and their French and British friends to know that the Germans had been so nervous, and to feel that Czechoslovakia was so strong that if she had mobilized she might have stopped the Austrian annexation. But it was not so comforting to reflect that the Germans had themselves believed that Czechoslovakia had reason to mobilize. In London the next day the British statesmen were "anxiously" considering what they would do about Czechoslovakia. While they considered, France and Soviet Russia, both of whom were bound by treaty to come to Czechoslovakia's aid if she were attacked,* declared that they would fulfill these engagements. The Germans solemnly told everyone that they wanted only peace with the Czechs. But on March 18 Litvinoff, the Soviet Russian Foreign Minister, declared that the seizure of Austria was an act of violence that endangered everyone, and he called

* See page 132.

for a conference of Great Britain, France, the United States and Russia to agree on ways for "checking the further development of aggression." All this time the British were still considering. On March 24 their Prime Minister, Mr. Neville Chamberlain, gave a speech in answer to this Russian proposal.

It was a vague and misty speech. Mr. Chamberlain had no desire to get mixed up with Bolshevist Russia in any such business. He had no desire to get Britain into a great war on the Continent. At the same time he did not want to see Adolf Hitler destroy Czechoslovakia and so open the way to the creation of a vast German empire in Eastern Europe, so powerful that it could terrorize the world. Mr. Chamberlain was a former business man, very reasonable, very conservative, very peaceable in his instincts; he did not want to see anybody do anything violent. Great Britain, he said in this speech, would not promise the Czechs beforehand that she would join with France and Russia in coming to their aid. At the same time, the Germans were not to believe that "nothing would make us fight." They must remember that if a war did break out in Central Europe, the British might very well come into it. But in the meanwhile, such a conference as Litvinoff had proposed would be just making trouble about something that might never happen; no one should take it for granted that any nation was planning to use force, and even to talk in that way was "bound to do harm."

Mr. Chamberlain clearly thought that it was still

possible to "make a deal with the dictators," as his policy came to be called. If everybody would be calm and reasonable and try to see each other's point of view, Germany and Italy on one side and France and Britain on the other could still work out some arrangement under which all would be satisfied; Bolshevist Russia would be pushed aside where she could no longer disturb European affairs and the Continent would return to peace and stability. He was just at this time negotiating a treaty with Italy intended to settle all the questions between them about Spain and the Near East and Ethiopia. He had accepted the annexation of Austria and shown that he would make no trouble with Germany about that. He was anxious that everything should not be upset now by a lot of unnecessary excitement over Czechoslovakia.

The thing to do was to avoid giving any promises to the Czechs that would lead them to take an extreme attitude. Instead they should be urged to do everything in their power to meet the just complaints of the Sudetens, in whom Hitler was so much interested. But Hitler should not be allowed to imagine that he could do what he pleased with Czechoslovakia as he had been permitted to do with Austria. Instead, he should be convinced that if he went too far, Britain would stand behind the Czechs; and thus he would be led to take a reasonable attitude on his own side. By following such a policy, one could hope that nobody would do anything rash, that something could be worked out and that peace would be the result. It was perhaps a good policy. The only trouble with it was that the Germany of Adolf Hitler had no intention of being either calm or reasonable, and had not the slightest interest in seeing Mr. Chamberlain's point of view—or any point of view except its own.

It was not even being honest. There can be no doubt that by this time Konrad Henlein, the leader of the Nazi-like Sudeten Germany party, was acting simply as an agent of Adolf Hitler, the ruler of a foreign power. But while his party paraded and saluted and shouted like the Nazis, he was careful never to say anything about the annexation of the Sudetens to Germany. Until the very last he pretended to act as a loyal citizen of Czechoslovakia, asking only to end the grievances and secure the just rights of its German-speaking minority but always without splitting up the country itself. Actually, the Sudetens of Czechoslovakia had been treated much better than any of the many other national minorities scattered through Europe, and vastly better than Nazi Germany was to treat the minorities which were to come into its power. They could not forget, however, that when their country was still a part of pre-war Austria-Hungary it was they who had held the power over the Czechs and not the other way around; they had suffered badly in the depression and had naturally blamed their troubles on the Czech government, and they did have real grievances which the Czechs had been rather slow to remedy. The trouble was that the more the Czechs now did toward removing these grievances, the more grievances Henlein thought up and the greater demands he made upon the Czech Republic.

Four days after Mr. Chamberlain's curious speech, the Czech government announced that it would propose a new law giving greater rights to the Sudetens. Henlein would have nothing to do with this, and about a month later he announced a program of eight demands of his own, going a long way beyond anything which had been asked before. They called for a formal division of the country into Czech and Sudeten areas; for full autonomy for the Sudeten area in every branch of public life, with all officials to be Sudetens; and for full freedom to the Sudetens to proclaim their "Germanism" and their German (which was to say, Nazi) political faith. And there was an additional demand. The Czech government must reverse its foreign policy, drop its alliances with France and Russia and so become a part of Hitler's political system. When one realizes that the Sudeten area was also the vital defense area of the country, and that Czechoslovakia was a democracy which was here asked to turn over this vital area to a disaffected minority, closely allied with a great dictatorship just over the border and left free to preach and practice dictatorship in its own autonomous government, it is easy to see how impossible it was for the Czechs to accept anything of the sort. They could not, they declared, negotiate these demands, but they would push forward their own program of reforms.

At this the newspapers and propaganda machinery within Germany broke out into a storm of abuse of the Czechs. Things began to look dangerous. Various prominent British statesmen made speeches, nervously hinting that Great Britain really might fight after all if things went too far. M. Daladier, the new Premier of France, hurried across the Channel on April 28 for a conference with Mr. Chamberlain. They agreed to bring the military plans of the two nations more closely into co-ordination; they agreed that France would live up to her treaty with Czechoslovakia if the Germans attacked; at the same time, they also agreed to urge Czechoslovakia to make all possible concessions. But they would not ask her to concede anything that would violate her democratic constitution or threaten her independence.

The British and French Ministers in Prague appeared at the Czech Foreign Office with messages to this effect. On the day they did so, Adolf Hitler was in Rome, returning the formal visit which Mussolini had made him the year before * in scenes of equal splendor and with even greater displays of military might and Italo-German friendship and unity. Matters drifted on for a few days. The Czechs were hard at work trying to devise some form of concession that would satisfy Henlein without writing a death-warrant for Czechoslovakia. Henlein was at work organizing a storm-troop corps of the familiar Nazi kind. The Berlin newspapers were denouncing the

* See page 181.

Czechs for having met not a single one of the Sudeten demands. Mr. Chamberlain was hoping for the best, but deciding—as he made plain to an American newspaper man at a private lunch which later became rather famous—that really there was not much that could be done about Czechoslovakia anyway. It was almost impossible for France and Russia to fight in defense of a country which was cut off from both of them; Mr. Chamberlain pretty clearly did not want to ask the British people to fight over this Central European question; perhaps the best way out would be to let Germany have the Sudeten area, leaving a "smaller but sounder" Czechoslovakia free of this internal dissension. But if Mr. Chamberlain really thought all this, he had not told the Czechs about it when suddenly, in the third week of May, rumors began to come of German Army divisions moving up to the Czechoslovak border.

President Beneš of Czechoslovakia had no intention of seeing his country swallowed suddenly without a fight, as Austria had been. He believed that if he showed force, his great allies would stand by him; to seem to challenge Hitler was dangerous, but to do nothing was more dangerous still. On Friday, May 20, the Czech Army was ordered to its war stations and specialists and one class of reserves were called to the colors. It was a crisis. The German press broke out in a fury over the reckless "violence" of the Czechs and fiercely denounced the British for "inciting" them to war. The French told Beneš that they would support him; the British indicated that they would stand by the French; the Russians would live up to their treaty and even the Poles gave their encouragement. Through Saturday and Sunday it looked as though Europe were actually on the verge of a great war. The Germans seemed to hesitate—and nothing happened. How much foundation there had been, if any, for the rumors of a troop concentration was uncertain.

There was no invasion. By the end of May the Czech reserves were being sent home again. Throughout the democratic countries it was being joyfully, perhaps a little boastfully, declared that for once the Nazis had met a show of force, and had immediately backed down. Perhaps they were really not so dangerous after all. The summer weather was coming; there were other things than Czechoslovakia to think about, and presently the French and British were busy with plans for a state visit which King George and Queen Elizabeth were to make to Paris in July—a visit which would be quite as grand as the dictators' receptions to each other and which would show that all the strength and solidarity was not on the side of the Axis.

The Czech problem seemed to be fading away. But there were still the troublesome negotiations over the rights of the Sudetens, which the Germans were certainly not making any easier. And there was something else. No one outside Germany knew it at the time. But one week after the May crisis, Adolf Hitler had given orders that there should be an immediate further increase in the German air forces and that every possible energy should be thrown into the task of bringing the great chain of fortifications along the French frontier—which had been under construction for some time—to completion. The Czech problem was not fading away.

The day before the British King and Queen were to leave for Paris, a certain Captain Wiedemann, who during the World War had commanded the company in which Adolf Hitler had served as a corporal and who was now a kind of confidential personal aid to the Nazi Führer, had a talk in London with Lord Halifax, the Foreign Secretary. As one of the royal party, Lord Halifax was in France next day, and there, among the parades and state dinners and celebrations, he had several long talks with the French statesmen. What they said to each other was not published. But not long after the King and Queen's return to England it was announced, on July 25, that Lord Runciman, a well-known figure in British politics, was to be sent on a special, but entirely "unofficial," mission to Czechoslovakia to act as a friendly and impartial mediator in the dispute between the Sudeten Germans and the Czech government.

Mr. Chamberlain explained this unusual move—in which a private individual was to be sent to meddle in the domestic affairs of another country—in his customarily vague way. Great Britain was anxious for an agreement between the Sudetens and the Czechs. But as time went on it seemed doubtful whether they could ever get together "without some assistance from the outside." Lord Runciman was going merely to investigate the whole affair and see if he could not suggest something to the two sides "which may help them," just as a mediator in an industrial strike tries to do. And, Mr. Chamberlain ended, "if only we could find a peaceful solution of this Czechoslovak question I should myself feel the way open again for a further effort for a general appeasement" in the whole of Europe.

Many people have wondered since whether Mr. Chamberlain really believed that Hitler would allow the Czech question to be settled in this way, and whether this was really all that Mr. Chamberlain had in mind. Many have asked whether the sending of Lord Runciman was not part of a rather different plan, which had perhaps been suggested by Captain Wiedemann and agreed upon with the French. They have wondered whether Mr. Chamberlain had not already decided that there was no way to prevent Hitler's taking the Sudeten areas except by a great war which would do far more damage than it could prevent; and that therefore the wisest course would be to let him annex the territory without opposition in the hope that he would then be satisfied and would be willing to work in a friendly way with the other great powers of Europe. They have wondered whether it was not Lord Runciman's real task to break down the Czech resistance to such a proposal, managing affairs so that the Czechs would not or could not call upon France and Russia to defend them under their treaties and thus precipitate a war. It was true that with the loss of the Sudeten area the Czechs would lose their one chance to defend themselves in the future. But if the Sudetens were transferred to Germany, Hitler would have no more reason or excuse for interfering with Czechoslovakia's affairs; the other powers could more safely guarantee what was left; and if a general "appeasement" should follow in Europe, the Czechs and Slovaks would be far better off and more secure than they could be in any other way.

Perhaps the Runciman mission was not really a part of any such plan as this, although from what followed it very well might have been. But if there was such a plan, Adolf Hitler, unfortunately, was not to show the slightest interest in helping to make it work out smoothly to "appeasement." Already the moment of calm after the May crisis had disappeared; again there was nervousness everywhere and all Europe was being filled with rumors. The Nazi press was hurling vituperation at the Czechs and exaggerating the "wrongs" and "tortures" of the Sudetens in more and more unmeasured terms. Reports were beginning to come out of Germany of extraordinary war measures being put into force. It was said that half a million laborers had been drafted and put frantically to work on the western fortifications. And the German Army maneuvers, which were to begin on August 15, were being planned on a scale which began to look more and more like mobilization and less and less like maneuvers. As Lord Runciman reached Prague on August 3, people in half a dozen capitals were quite seriously laying bets as to whether the 15th of the month would prove "the Day" scheduled for the start of a second great European war.

It was not; August 15 passed and nothing happened, but there was no lessening of the tension. As German reserves were called up by the hundred thousand for the "maneuvers" and Hitler set out on tour of his armies, the French began to call up their own reserves, and the British Fleet was ordered to be ready to take its war stations. The French statesmen were still assuring the Czechs that they would stand by them; the British were still making vague public pronouncements, explaining how much they wanted peace but warning the world not to imagine that they might not fight. In Prague Lord Runciman was busy, seeing the Czechs, seeing rather more of the Sudetens, urging fresh "concessions." The Czechs embodied these suggestions in a so-called "third plan" for Sudeten autonomy and offered it to Henlein. Henlein promptly flew to Berchtesgaden to consult Hitler.

So the pretense was at last being dropped that all this was just a matter between the Czech government and its German-speaking citizens; with Lord Runciman's assistance it was being transformed into an issue between Czechoslovakia and Nazi Germany, which was a very different affair. Henlein came back with

Hitler's rejection of the "third plan"; it would have to be the eight-point program demanded in June, or nothing. One of the minor Sudeten leaders announced in a speech that there could be no compromise and that the Sudetens now had "76,000,000 Germans behind them." President Beneš and his Cabinet worked out a "fourth plan," going farther than anything offered before, probably going far beyond the point of safety for Czechoslovakia's future. But it would show France and Britain that the Czechs had done everything in their power for peace, and leave the great democracies with no excuse for not coming to Czechoslovakia's assistance if Germany insisted on forcing a crisis.

This "fourth plan" was handed to the Sudeten leaders on September 6. On the following day the vast annual party demonstration of the German Nazis was to open at Nuremberg. It was to last through a week of parades and oratory, with Hitler scheduled to make one of his decisive speeches on the closing day. Without even waiting for the text of the "fourth plan" Henlein flew to Nuremberg to stay as Hitler's guest. The whole world was now watching this gathering for a sign of what was to happen. And as it opened on the morning of September 7 a famous editorial appeared in the London *Times*—the great newspaper which was everywhere regarded as the mouthpiece of the Chamberlain government—suggesting that perhaps the best solution of the Czech question would be the annexation of the Sudeten area to Germany.

So Great Britain, people everywhere thought at once, was going to let the Czechs down after all. The government denied that this was its policy, but the whole effort to create the impression that unless the Germans were reasonable France and Britain would fight had been badly shaken. The Sudeten leaders suddenly broke off the negotiations with the Czech government over the "fourth plan." At Nuremberg, the fiery oratory flowed on. In Czechoslovakia, the Henlein storm troops were now inciting all sorts of disorders and riots—the old, familiar method for creating a situation in which German troops would have to intervene "to restore order." And then at Nuremberg on the evening of September 12 came Hitler's speech, a single frenzied voice shouting and screaming through the radios of the world against the deep background of the rhythmic, roaring "Sieg Heil, Sieg Heil, Sieg Heils" of the vast party crowd.

He poured out an astonishingly vituperative attack upon "the liar Beneš and the criminal government at Prague." They had, he shouted, "invented the lie that Germany had mobilized troops and was about to invade Czechoslovakia" in May; he raged at "the Jewish fabricators of these press lies" who "hoped to bring about war by this means." Recklessly he exaggerated the situation in Czechoslovakia; the Sudetens, he declared, "are being oppressed in an inhuman and intolerable manner . . . brutally struck . . .

terrorized or maltreated . . . pursued like wild
beasts for every expression of their national life." He
went on:

And I say that if these tortured creatures cannot obtain rights and assistance by themselves,
they can obtain both from us. An end must be
made of depriving these people of their rights.
. . . I demand that the oppression of 3,500,000
Germans in Czechoslovakia shall cease and be
replaced by the free right of self-determination.

"Self-determination" meant far more than minority rights or autonomy or anything that Henlein had
been pretending to ask. It meant that the Sudetens
should be free to break up the Czechoslovak state if
they wished. And if they were not given that right,
Germany would intervene by force and get it for
them.

Here was an appalling situation. In Czechoslovakia
there was rioting, answered by martial law and the
issuance of a warrant for Konrad Henlein's arrest for
high treason. If Mr. Chamberlain had hoped quietly
and peaceably to engineer the transfer of the Sudeten
areas to Germany, Hitler had now destroyed the
hope. He had brought the whole Continent to a state
of intense excitement, with probably several million
men standing ready under arms, with everywhere the
fierce atmosphere of war. He was in effect demanding the transfer of the Sudetens under the direct
threat of force. For France and Britain to yield under

these conditions would be something very different from handing over the Sudetens under a friendly, agreed "solution." It would be a terrific blow to French and British prestige; it would prove them helpless to protect small allies even when they were bound by treaty to do so; it would make it infinitely more difficult for them to put any barriers in the way of Hitler's seemingly unlimited ambitions. It would imperil their own safety. But the only way to avoid yielding was immediately to threaten Hitler with war —a war which would be very difficult to fight, which no one wanted, and which would probably begin by wrecking Czechoslovakia anyway. The French Cabinet was divided and uncertain. British policy was in the hands of Mr. Chamberlain. And Mr. Chamberlain now acted upon a remarkable plan which he had already been thinking of as a last resort. To Adolf Hitler at Berchtesgaden he sent a personal message: "In view of the increasingly critical situation, I propose to come over at once to see you with the view of trying to find a peaceful solution."

To millions in the various countries who already felt themselves on the ragged edge of a great war, it was a striking and dramatic gesture. Early on the morning of Thursday, September 15, the elderly, lanky Prime Minister, with his wing collar and famous rolled umbrella, climbed into an airplane and was swept off through the skies to Germany, like an awkward angel of peace and reasonableness. For three hours that same evening he sat with Hitler in his mountain house at Berchtesgaden; he was back in England next day and an announcement said that there would be further discussions. All over the world people applauded what seemed the one sensible and direct move in an otherwise insane situation. Mr. Chamberlain had gained time; and he had gained for himself a much more complete control over the negotiations on the democratic side. But he had gained little else. Hitler had been polite, but had told the Englishman flatly that the Sudetens must have the right of self-determination, and made it so plain that he was resolved to invade the country at once that Chamberlain "asked him why he had allowed me to travel all that way, since I was evidently wasting my time." Hitler's answer was that if Great Britain would not agree to self-determination, there was no use of any further talking. Chamberlain said that he could not break off negotiations in that way without consulting his government. The one concession he got from the Nazi dictator was a promise that there would be no invasion of Czechoslovakia until he had time to do so.

The crowds who cheered Mr. Chamberlain as a peacemaker when he came back to London did not know anything of this. They did not know that the Prime Minister had meekly decided that self-determination for the Sudetens—which of course meant the break-up of Czechoslovakia—was "the sole hope of a peaceful solution." Peaceful, that is to say, for everyone except Czechoslovakia. They did not know that all the hurried comings and goings of the next few anxious days were devoted solely to getting the Czech government to accept this surrender, without resisting by arms and so starting the war in which the French and British would then have to join. Early on Sunday morning, September 18, Premier Daladier of France and his Foreign Minister arrived in London and all that day were in consultation with the British. In the evening the news of their decision was out, and at two o'clock next afternoon, France and Great Britain formally called upon the Czech government to hand over to Hitler all of its territory in which even as many as half the inhabitants were Sudeten Germans. "They have condemned my country," cried the Czech minister in Paris, "without a hearing!" The shocked statesmen in Prague called it "the basest betrayal in history."

It was a betrayal of the French treaty pledges to Czechoslovakia and of the assurances with which Great Britain had backed them up. It amounted to opening all Southeastern Europe to possible German aggression. It meant paralyzing the excellent Czech Army, whose forty well-equipped divisions would be missing now from the democratic side if a great war ever should come to Europe. Mr. Chamberlain and the French statesmen who agreed with him have been bitterly condemned for it. But there is another side. A great war was bound to be a terrible alternative. Even at this point, if the sacrifice were made it was still possible that a real appeasement might result.

For there was one striking thing about all the negotiations. The Russians, whose aid would be absolutely
essential if a fight was to be made for Czechoslovakia,
had barely even been consulted. The British and many
of the French feared and distrusted the Russians—and
perhaps with more reason, as later events have indicated, than was realized at the time. By following
Mr. Chamberlain's policy the two democracies would
be freed of this awkward ally, whom Hitler and
Mussolini professed so much to hate. A real "deal"
with the Nazi and Fascist dictators ought to be made
much easier. A new working European system might
thus at last be set up. And it was even possible that
if the Nazis continued to be aggressive, they could be
led to turn their warlike ambitions against Russia,
and these two kinds of unpleasant dictatorship might
finally destroy each other in a struggle between
them. Was any democratic statesman justified in risk-
ing all the horrors of a great war in view of such
alternative possibilities?

The Czech government struggled against the hard
decision. The British and French note had been received on Monday, the 19th; it would have to be accepted before Wednesday, the 21st, when Mr. Chamberlain was again to see Herr Hitler. The Czechs refused to accept, in a really fine and moving document.
The British and French suppressed it; and at quarter
past two on Wednesday morning the French and
British Ambassadors at Prague routed President Beneš
out of bed to tell him, in effect, that he must accept,

and that if he did not, he could not hope to get any military aid from France and Britain. At an early morning cabinet meeting the Czech government decided that it could only yield. Under certain conditions it agreed to do as its great allies demanded.

Delayed by one day, Mr. Chamberlain took to the air again on Thursday, the 22nd, to meet Hitler at the town of Godesberg on the Rhine. The Czechs had given up; they had agreed to cede all territories with 50 per cent or more of Sudetens; the crisis should have been over. To his surprise Mr. Chamberlain found that it was only beginning. Instead of accepting the Czech surrender and working out orderly details for a peaceful transfer, Hitler announced that the German Army must immediately occupy the Sudeten territory as he defined it himself on a map; that there must be plebiscites to decide the fate of additional areas, and that the troops must march by October 1, a bare week away. Chamberlain protested. Hitler worked himself into one of his famous rages. The situation of the Sudetens was "unbearable," he said, "and must be terminated by me." To the shocked Prime Minister this was not peace or appeasement; it was brute dictation and war. Chamberlain, as one writer says, "had come to Godesberg determined to have peace at almost any price. It looked as though Hitler were determined to have war at almost any price." To yield under such peremptory orders as this, after they had already yielded so much, would put the democracies in so weak a position as

to destroy the whole value of the settlement as a
foundation for peace. Chamberlain did not know
whether the Czechs could be forced to take these
additional demands; he did not know whether his
own public would accept them when it learned what
was really happening. Before Chamberlain left Godesberg the Czechs had been told that France and Britain would no longer advise them not to mobilize; and
the Czech mobilization orders had gone out.

There followed a few strange days of frantic negotiation and of a brave but eleventh-hour show of
force. The British Fleet was fully mobilized. The
French called another half-million reserves to the
colors. Gas masks were hurriedly passed out to the
British people and in London and Paris workmen began digging air-raid shelter trenches through the
beautiful parks. In Prague the people stood grimly
ready, glancing at the skies with the thought that at
any moment they might be filled with the roar of the
Nazi bombers. Great Britain and France simply
passed on the new demands of Hitler to the Czechs,
without advising them to accept, and at the same time
published the text. A report went around that the
Germans would not wait until the coming Saturday,
October 1, but would march at two o'clock on Wednesday afternoon. On Monday evening Hitler made
another roaring speech, heaping violent abuse upon
the Czechs, in the huge Sport Palace in Berlin. The
British definitely told the French, for the first time,
that if Germany attacked Czechoslovakia, Great Brit-

ain would fight; and a public statement by the British
Foreign Office declared that Britain and Russia would
both stand by France. So the democracies were now
calling the Russians back upon the scene from which
Mr. Chamberlain's policy had excluded them.

On Tuesday evening there was a grave radio address by Mr. Chamberlain; it was serious, but it was
still a little vague. The French and British had reached
the position that if Hitler would agree to negotiate
peaceably, they would see that the Sudeten area was
handed over; but that if he tried to take it by force
they would fight. It may seem a small difference over
which to decide the question of peace or war, and
yet in a way it did express the fundamental issue—
was Europe to be organized into a working system
in which the relations of the powers could be settled
by discussion, or was it to be dominated by unre-
strained force against which nobody would be safe?
Hitler was insisting that he would march into
Czechoslovakia on October 1. The French and British people were preparing themselves to fight. But
then, at the very last minute, the Nazi Führer suddenly agreed that if Mr. Chamberlain and M. Daladier wanted to discuss the matter, he would be willing to have a discussion.

Mr. Chamberlain had called the British Parliament
to meet on Wednesday afternoon, the 28th. It gathered in a very serious mood. War seemed almost certain; and as Mr. Chamberlain began a long and somber
account of everything that had happened, the cer-

tainty seemed only to deepen. But as the Prime Minister was reaching the latter part of his speech, there
was a sudden little stir in the House; a paper was
handed up to the speaker; he paused, read it, and
then announced that Hitler had invited him to a
conference at Munich next day, together with Daladier for France and Mussolini for Italy. "I need not
say," he went on, "what my answer will be."

It was a tremendously dramatic moment. To all
these men, sitting there in the expectation that war
would be upon them and bombs perhaps raining
down on London within a few days or hours, it
seemed that peace had suddenly and miraculously
dawned. They did not stop to ask how a conference
would change matters or what would be discussed.
They were overwhelmed with relief and enthusiasm;
so were the crowds outside; so were the throngs at
the airport next morning as Mr. Chamberlain took off
for Munich with the happy parting word that "it's
all right this time." For the third time Mr. Chamberlain roared away. By one o'clock on that Thursday,
the 29th, he was in Munich with the heads of the
three other powers, and they were sitting together in
the "Brown House," the central headquarters of
Hitler's Nazi party. But no representatives of Czechoslovakia, whose fate they were deciding, were sitting
with them. The French and British had their peaceable negotiation. But when, early on Friday morning,
the results were handed out, it was not easy to see
what had been negotiated. Hitler had agreed to oc-

cupy the territory he had demanded by stages instead of all in one jump. There were some weak provisions —they were never carried out—for international supervision over the details of the settlement. But Hitler was given just what he had said he would take; and the German Army rolled, unopposed, across the Czechoslovak boundary promptly on October 1, as he had said that it would.

It was a complete surrender by the British and French. There is a story that when Daladier, flying home from Munich, saw a vast crowd waiting on the Paris airport, he told his pilot to circle the field before landing as he was afraid they were there to lynch him. The story is probably not true, but it might have been. When he did land they mobbed him with joy, as a hero and peacemaker. When Mr. Chamberlain stepped from his plane it was to thunderous applause of British crowds. He brought, he told them "peace with honor. I believe it is peace for our time." They cheered him again and again. Not only in France and Great Britain but in Germany as well Mr. Chamberlain was hailed for a few days with an emotion which showed how deep the fear of war had really been. But he had not brought "peace for our time"; and he had brought a surrender which was only temporarily concealed by the way in which the events of the final days had been staged.

Perhaps, as some believe, he had intended it all along. Perhaps he could not have helped himself. Once France and Britain had forced Czechoslovakia to agree to give over the Sudeten area, they had made it almost impossible to reverse the policy, in spite of all their mobilizations and warlike gestures, when Hitler contrived to make the annexation so much worse a diplomatic defeat for them than they had intended. But also, perhaps, France and Britain could not have faced a war in the fall of 1938. In abandoning Czechoslovakia they lost the forty divisions of the Czech Army, they lost the "little Maginot Line," and they opened the military resources of the Southeast to Germany. But if they had fought at that time they would have been obliged to rely heavily on Russian aid—and they not only distrusted the Russians' intentions but had great doubts of their military efficiency. And only after the Czech crisis was over did it become clear how weak their own defenses really were, how far both countries had been behind Germany in aviation and anti-aircraft defenses and modern weapons. Though he came back bearing "peace," Mr. Chamberlain immediately set in motion a tremendous increase in the British rearmament effort, and as this work got under way in the following year it showed more and more plainly how much had been neglected. Perhaps Mr. Chamberlain could not help himself.

But it was a heavy defeat. As the crowds cheered in London, the German armies rolled on through the Sudetenland, with the Czech soldiers sullenly retreating and with crowds of Jews, liberals, anti-Nazi Germans—many of whom had taken refuge in

Czechoslovakia from other advances of the swastika—
frantically flying before them while yet there was
time. The Hitler shadow was spreading. At Munich,
Britain and France had declared that they would give
what was left of Czechoslovakia a guarantee of its
safety and independence. After what had just happened, everyone knew that it would not be worth the
paper it was written on. Hitler had given Mr. Chamberlain a declaration that it was "the desire of our
two peoples never to go to war again." It was the one
definite bit of "appeasement" that the British Prime
Minister had got from his policy; and few thought
that was worth the paper it was written on either.

11. THE END OF APPEASEMENT

THE BRITISH AND FRENCH HAD THEIR
moment of enormous relief. The crowds cheered the
peace and the peacemakers. Mr. Chamberlain looked
forward at last to the beginning of that general "appeasement" for which he had sacrificed so much.
"We can thus hope," said Premier Daladier, explain-

ing it all to the French Parliament, "to substitute the practices of right for the solutions of force"; and, indeed, in December von Ribbentrop, the Nazi Foreign Minister, paid a formal visit to Paris to sign a declaration of friendship with France like that which Hitler at Munich had signed with Chamberlain. But he passed through empty streets to an icy reception. Even by that time it was beginning to be clear just what kind of "appeasement" had actually been bought at Munich.

The first shock had come on October 9, when Hitler returned from his triumphant entry into the Sudetenland to make a speech at Saarbruecken, on the French frontier. It was in the Führer's characteristic, and anything but peaceful, manner. He boasted of the armed strength of Germany and announced the new expansions of the German Army and air force which he was putting into effect. He scolded the British, practically ordered them not to replace Mr. Chamberlain with any of their more anti-German politicians on pain of war, and rudely advised them, so far as Germany was concerned, to mind their own business. It was not a good beginning for a new reign of friendship. Nor were the shocking scenes which took place in Germany when, early in November, a young Jewish refugee in Paris shot and killed one of the diplomats attached to the German Embassy.

For some fourteen hours gangs of Nazi thugs and storm troopers ranged through the German cities,

wrecking and looting Jewish shops, setting fire to
synagogues, maiming or beating Jews and rounding
them up by the hundred for shipment to the concentration camps. It was pretended that this was a "spon-
taneous" outburst of popular anger, finally put down
by the police; but Goebbels, the little Propaganda
Minister, declared that it showed "healthy instincts,"
and it was followed by the announcement of a coldly
official program for stripping the Jews of what prop-
erty was left to them and destroying or driving them
from the country. A "fine" of a billion marks was
imposed upon the Jewish community as retribution
for the Paris assassination; thousands of Jews were
simply dumped across the border into Poland, without money or possessions, and the democratic countries everywhere found themselves confronted with
fresh hordes of helpless and penniless refugees. The
problem of these quite innocent victims of Nazism
was an exasperating one all through the winter and
spring; and it did not lessen the suspicion, the fear
and the hostility of France and Britain toward a
government which could regard such brutalities as
the sign of "healthy instincts."

The war in Spain, in the meanwhile, was dragging
savagely on; but it was clearer every day that the end
was coming and that the end would be a complete
victory for General Franco and his Axis allies.
Would Mussolini really get out of the country, as
he had so often said he would, when it was all over?
It hardly seemed so. Instead, Italian propaganda was

now pressing old claims to Tunisia—a French colony in North Africa largely settled by Italians—and Italian crowds were being encouraged to shout, not only for Tunisia, but for the French island of Corsica and even for the French provinces of Nice and Savoy. Italian troops were being marched and counter-marched along the border of Tunisia, and were threatening Egypt. In January Mr. Chamberlain anxiously took up his rolled umbrella again and set off for Rome; the conversations with the Italian dictator seem to have been polite, but little came of them. Then Barcelona, the last important base for the Spanish government armies, fell; in Rome, Mussolini appeared upon his balcony to address a huge crowd in celebration of the event. "Our enemies are biting the dust!" And the crowd roared back: "Tunisia! Corsica! Nice and Savoy!"

Was this appeasement? Or did it mean that after the smashing blows just delivered from the Berlin end of the Axis, the Rome end was now to have its turn? Everywhere in Europe the chimneys of the arms factories were smoking only more and more furiously; everywhere huge armies were drilling; everywhere citizens of the great capitals were being solemnly trained to protect themselves against a murderous destruction that might at any time be let fall from the skies into the midst of their daily lives; everywhere the immense, controlled propaganda machines of the dictator states were concealing facts from their own peoples and filling the air with vio-

lence, passion and half-truths, while the democratic
press was more and more passionately answering
back. In the first days of the new year the wildest
rumors began to go about, and—when there was so
much threatening secrecy on every side—no one
could ever be quite sure that they were not true. It
was rumored that Hitler was about to attack in the
east, or attack in the west; it was rumored that he
would now back up Mussolini in an attack on
France; it was even rumored that Nazi Germany
was about to come together with Communist Russia
in an attack upon the world. But that, after all the
diatribes that Hitler and the Communists had hurled
at each other, seemed too fantastic.

In this poisonous atmosphere it began to seem as
though something more would have to be done to
get appeasement than simply to wait for it. Premier
Daladier felt driven to answer the threats coming
from Italy with a strong statement in the Chamber
of Deputies. France, he said, "will not concede a
single acre or concede a single right" to threats of
force; and the Chamber broke into cheers. On January 28—two days before Hitler was scheduled to
make a speech celebrating the sixth anniversary of
the Nazi régime—Mr. Chamberlain tried his hand.
Great Britain, he declared, was ready to satisfy any
"reasonable" desires of Italy or Germany, so far as
it could do so, but would refuse to negotiate under
any "demand to dominate the world by force." It
was time for the Axis powers to make some "con-

tribution" from their side to the general peace which everyone talked about. Two days later the world listened with some interest to hear whether Hitler would do so. He did not.

However, he did not actually threaten anyone with war. The speech was as violent in its language as usual, but even more vague, and to a Europe which was getting accustomed to Hitler speeches it seemed distinctly moderate. The wild rumors began to die away. The Italians ceased to shout for Tunisia and Corsica. The arms factories were humming louder than ever; the armies and air forces grew bigger; nothing had been settled in any way, but for a month or so there was a kind of lull. And then in the first days of March there began to come reports of fresh troubles in what had been left of Czechoslovakia.

After the Sudeten territories had been cut off, there remained the Czechs, who occupied the western half of the country, their close relatives, the Slovaks, who lived in the center, and the much smaller and more backward group of Ruthenians in the mountainous eastern "tail." The Slovaks and Ruthenians had always been restless under the dominant position held by the Czechs; and in the general smash-up caused by Munich each had secured autonomous governments of their own under the central government of Prague. It was not a stable arrangement. After Munich President Beneš had resigned and left the country, where he would no longer have been safe from the Germans; his successor, President Emil Hacha, left to struggle between the pressure constantly put upon him by Berlin and the agitation in Slovakia and Ruthenia, which the Germans were doing much to encourage, found the country going to pieces in his hands. There was an anti-Semitic, Nazi-like storm-troop organization, the Hlinka Guard, in Slovakia; there was separatist conspiracy, actively encouraged from Germany, in the Slovak government; there was trouble in Ruthenia. President Hacha began to take energetic measures to prevent the break-up of what was left of the country. The Ruthenian government was made over; and on March 10 the Slovak premier, Joseph Tiso, was dismissed with some of his ministers, the Hlinka Guard was ordered to be disarmed and several of its leaders were arrested.

It was also on March 10, as it happened, that Josef Stalin appeared before a Communist party congress in Moscow to deliver a striking and rather curious speech. The Russian dictator was very severe about Great Britain, France and their Munich policy of appeasement—much more severe than he was toward Germany and Italy, who were Russia's declared enemies. The whole policy of the democracies, he implied, was "not to interfere with and prevent aggressors from committing their black deeds"—particularly not to prevent Germany or Japan from "getting tied up in war with the Soviet Union." Russia, on the other hand, was interested solely in peace; and one of Russia's tasks was to be cautious and "not allow ourselves to be drawn into conflicts with the provokers of war who are accustomed to make others rake their chestnuts out of the fire." From the way in which the democratic press and politicians talked, "one might think the Germans were given districts of Czechoslovakia as a bribe to begin a war against the Soviet Union." This sounded very threatening toward the democracies. But after all, a great many people had thought just that; it was not unnatural that Stalin should be annoyed about the Munich affair, and other passages in his speech seemed to make it clear that he was still on the side of the democracies against the Nazi-Fascist Axis. And the speech, moreover, was quickly overshadowed by what was now happening in Czechoslovakia.

March 10 was a Friday. On Saturday, the Hlinka Guards were in the streets in Bratislava, the Slovak capital; there was a series of minor riots there during the day, while the German radio station in Vienna poured out a steady stream of propaganda for Slovakian independence. Sunday passed more quietly, but the nervous leaders in Prague heard of heavy German troop concentrations on the border opposite Bratislava. On Monday, Dr. Tiso, the dismissed Slovakian premier, crossed into German territory, took an airplane for Berlin and was received by Hitler the same evening. In Bratislava, while he was on his way, there was a demonstration for independence; crowds of Germans and Slovaks were shouting "Sieg Heil!" and "Heil Hitler!" and during the afternoon and evening the city was rocked by a series of thunderous bomb explosions, manufacturing —at a cost of half a dozen killed and many wounded —the appearance of "disorder" which would serve as an excuse for an invasion.

At midnight a voice over the Vienna radio was heard shouting in Slovak: "In a few hours a thousand years' dream will be fulfilled and we will have an independent Slovak state." At Berlin, in the early hours of Tuesday, the 14th, it was reported that in answer to Tiso's appeal a German ultimatum had been served on the Prague government and that Hitler's troops would march on the following morning. The German press was now dripping with stories of riots and outrages in Czechoslovakia; all that Tuesday the Berlin radio was filling the air with bloodcurdling tales of "atrocities" being committed by Czechs against Germans. The old invention about Communists running wild in police uniforms was dragged out; the Czech police was represented as having "lost control." By afternoon President Hacha and his Foreign Minister, in answer to a strong suggestion from the Germans, were "voluntarily" on their way to Berlin. Their train, delayed by troop trains headed for their country, did not arrive until half past ten Tuesday evening. At the station, the Czechs found themselves received with the utmost ceremony and politeness. There was a military guard of honor for them; there was a band; they were formally escorted to one of the leading Berlin hotels.

But they were given no rest. They were barely in-
stalled in their rooms before the Nazi Foreign Minister, von Ribbentrop, arrived to confront them with
the demand that they must sign away the last shred
of Czechoslovak independence.

At Munich, France and Great Britain had
"pledged themselves," as Premier Daladier put it,
"immediately and without reservations" to guarantee
the safety of what was left of the Czechoslovak
Republic. They had never done so. As this frantic
Tuesday wore on, what were the French and British
doing? Nothing. Someone put a question about it to
Mr. Chamberlain in the House of Commons. "The
proposed guarantee," he lamely answered, "was one
against unprovoked aggression. No such aggression
has yet taken place." President Hacha, standing alone
at midnight against von Ribbentrop's pounding arguments, could hardly have felt the same way about it.
At one o'clock Wednesday morning the Czech
President and Foreign Minister were finally conducted across the street to confront Hitler himself
in his vast and gorgeous new Chancellery. Again
there was a military guard, ironically presenting arms
for the wretched men; again there was a band playing in their honor. They disappeared into the
building.

As in the case of Schuschnigg's fatal visit to
Berchtesgaden * there are many stories of the ordeal
that followed, of the browbeatings, threats and pres-

* See page 193.

sures to which they were subjected. But for three
hours, at least, Hacha stood his ground; it was not
until 4:15 that morning that the conference was over
and a communiqué announced that President Hacha
had signed his country's death-warrant. "The
Czechoslovak President," it said, with a particularly
cruel hypocrisy, "declared that in order to assure
[peace and order] he trustfully laid the fate of the
Czech people and country into the hands of the
German Reich." He could do nothing else. Already
200,000 German troops were pouring across the
borders. Hitler issued a proclamation: "In Bohemia
and Moravia [the two Czech provinces] intolerable
terror reigned against the German national comrades.
Units of the German Army and Air Force will
therefore march into Czech state territory. I expect
of every German soldier that he will not consider
himself an enemy of the inhabitants." But, the
Führer went on, "wherever the advance meets opposition, it must be crushed immediately and with all
means." There was no pretense that President Hacha
had any legal power to sign away his country's existence. There was no pretense at investigation, at
allowing to the Czechs the principle of self-determination about which Hitler had talked so much at
Munich, at anything, in fact, except a brute seizure
of a helpless country. At 4:30 in the morning the
authorities in Prague broadcast an appeal to the
Czech people not to attempt a resistance which
would be hopeless. At about the same time President

Hacha and his Foreign Minister were returning, worn out, to their Berlin hotel. They found their rooms tastefully banked with flowers—the gift of the Nazi government.

All that Wednesday morning, the 15th, German troops were rolling across what had been Czechoslovakia. Late the same afternoon Hitler himself reached Prague, and that evening the sullen Czechs saw the Nazi Führer's standard floating over their ancient Hradschin Castle, symbolizing the end of their national life. It was one year, exactly, since Hitler had made his entry into Vienna; it was a bare five days—so brutally sudden was the stroke—since the dismissal of Tiso had provided Hitler with his opportunity.

The democratic countries were shocked, frightened and appalled. With one brusque movement Hitler had torn up the whole Munich settlement. The last shred of pretense that it was a peace which had been made there had been destroyed. Hitler had proved already that he would not be bound by treaties; he was now proving that he would not be bound even by his own declared principles. He had always pretended before that he wanted only to bring those of German race under the Nazi flag; here he had ruthlessly seized some 10,000,000 non-Germans and bound them to the gun-wheels of his huge military empire. What would he do next? Where would it end? What limits were there for an ambition which had refused to be limited by inter-

national law, by treaties, by pledges, by its own
professed aims, even by its own principles? For a
time the men who had made the Munich "settlement" hesitated. Mr. Chamberlain was inclined to

GERMANY AND AUSTRIA-HUNGARY: 1914

feel that nothing could be done; that the whole business was unfortunate, but that it ought not to turn
the democracies back from their search after appeasement. The shock, however, was too much. Two days
after Hitler's standard had been hoisted over the
Hradschin Castle, Mr. Chamberlin went before an
audience in his native city of Birmingham, and as he

reviewed everything that had happened, there was no mistaking the bitterness and disillusion in his tone. Hitler, in spite of all that the democracies had sacrificed, in spite of all his promises, all his assurances,

CENTRAL EUROPE: 1939

had "now taken the law into his own hands. . . . Is this the end of an old adventure or is it the beginning of a new? . . . Is this in fact a step in the direction of an attempt to dominate the world by force?" And a couple of days after Mr. Chamberlain spoke, Premier Daladier went before the French Senate to ask special emergency powers:

The present circumstances call less for
speeches than for action. . . . We are now in
the trench which we must defend at the cost of
whatever sacrifice. The Munich agreement? Destroyed. The mutual declaration of Franco-German collaboration [signed with von Ribbentrop in December]? Violated in letter and spirit.
. . . Today, and in the hours to come, we shall
have to face events that may develop danger-
ously. . . . This is the storm, gentlemen, and
we must face it with all the means the situation
requires and with our will and the will of the
people of France.

It was the end of appeasement. The democracies
had had enough.

12. WAR

IT WAS THE END OF APPEASEMENT. Perhaps it need not have been the end of peace. It may be said that in a sense there was no "reason," in the spring of 1939, for another great European war. There were no vast, mechanical "causes" driving the nations to battle, in the same way that the wind drives the leaves before it, or that drought and famine once caused populations to migrate over the earth. There was no struggle for "survival." People were not starving to death in any of the great powers; and even if they had been, there was no possibility that by fighting a major war they could seize the food they needed. There were no resources which even the poorest of the European peoples could hope to conquer in such a war that they could not have got the use of much more cheaply and easily in other ways. On any sensible, practical, dollars-and-cents basis it was quite certain that the costs of a great war would far outrun anything that anyone could hope to gain by it.

Some of the nations, to be sure, were richer and

more prosperous than others; a war might distribute
the prosperity somewhat differently, but the one
thing which seemed sure was that in doing so it was
bound to impoverish all. None of the nations, at the
same time, was too well off; the economic systems of
all of them—both democratic and dictatorial—were
on a pretty shaky basis, and all of them faced many
serious problems. But most people, even in the dictatorial countries, were deeply convinced that large-
scale war never settles any problems. Clearly, the
great war of 1914-1918 had not done so; it had only
made them worse. Another great war would probably only make them worse than ever. Certainly in
the spring of 1939 there was no European people who
wanted a war; and it seems almost as certain that
there was no national leader—not even Hitler or
Mussolini or Stalin—who wanted another great war
like that of 1914.

And yet another great war came. It did not come
for any one "reason," but because of everything
which had gone before. It came because it turned out
that—after all the fears and hatreds and violences of
the years since 1918, after all the vacillations and
uncertainties of the democratic powers and all the
brutal but successful vigor of the dictators, after all
the piling up of armaments, all the shrieking insults
and half truths and fantastic theories of the propaganda machines, and all the familiarity with the idea
of war which these things left behind them—after all
this, there was simply no way in which the knobbly

building blocks of the European nations could be put together into a stable and working system without a war. It came, very largely, because Adolf Hitler was the kind of man he was, and because he thought and acted as he did. It came because of what he had done, because of the kind of ideas in which he believed and in which he had taught the German people—or at least his Nazi party dictatorship—to believe. From beginning to end, his was the most active part; he was the man who, more than any one other, did dangerous things when they might have been left undone, who failed to do the reasonable and conciliatory things when he might have done them, who took the risks and forced the pace and who must bear the greatest responsibility in any ordinary meaning of that word.

Yet it also came because Chamberlain and Daladier and their advisers were the kind of men they were and because of the kind of ideas in which their peoples believed. It came because the democratic statesmen surrendered when they might have been firm and because they did not dare surrender when firmness could no longer prevent a war. Theirs was a much less direct responsibility. It can be said that if, in the spring of 1939, Germany had suddenly passed into the hands of some other kind of government there might well have been no war; it cannot be said in the same way that if Britain and France had passed into different hands there would have been no war. But at bottom the war came because over the years a

situation had been created—whoever was most responsible for it—of fear, jealousy and hatred, of tremendous armaments ready to be used, of directly conflicting ideas between which there was no ground
for compromise. No "balance" of these forces had
been possible. In all this there was no practical
"reason" for a war. But it made a war extremely
likely. No one planned or wanted the war. But in the
end there was no way out. Given everything that
had gone before, there was, in the steps by which
the war was now in fact to come, something almost
accidental. Perhaps this means that it need not have
happened. Or perhaps it means that by this time a
war had been made inevitable.

One week after the destruction of Czechoslovakia,
the blow suddenly fell upon the little Republic of
Lithuania. Its chief city and only seaport, Memel,
had belonged to Germany before the World War,
and was still largely inhabited by Germans. Hitler
demanded its return, and got it—for Lithuania had
no choice. And at the same time he laid before
Poland his proposed "solution" for the controversy
over Danzig and the Polish Corridor—one of the oldest controversies left over by the 1919 treaties. The
treaties, in order to give the new Polish state the out-
let to the sea which was believed essential if the
country was to survive, had cut the "corridor" out
of German territory, and had made the very German
seaport of Danzig, at the mouth of Poland's great
river, a "free city" in which Poland was to enjoy

certain commercial and customs rights. To Germans, this had always been one of the most bitterly resented arrangements of the peace. Hitler now demanded that Danzig be restored to Germany and that Germany be given a strip of territory across the Corridor to East Prussia wide enough for a motor road and railway.

In more normal times, and if it had come from a more ordinary sort of government, this solution, considering everything, might not have seemed unreasonable. Yet, no matter how narrow the ceded strip might be, it would mean giving Nazi Germany a barrier completely across Poland's only avenue to the sea. With the fate of Czechoslovakia immediately before them, with so many other examples in mind of Hitler's terrible and irresistible method of piecemeal attack, and with many already predicting that after Czechoslovakia it would be "Poland's turn next," the Poles had reason to believe that meekly to accept these proposals would be the beginning of the end of their independence. Instead of accepting, they sent back proposals of their own. To these there was no reply.

Was there about to be still another violent revision of the map of Europe? And if so, what were the great democracies to do? In 1934 Poland had signed a ten-year nonaggression treaty with the Nazis,* which ought to have protected her, but no one could now suppose that treaties would mean anything to

* See pages 107 and 173.

Hitler. What were Mr. Chamberlain and M. Daladier to do? They could do nothing—and presently see Poland swallowed up in the Nazi empire as Czechoslovakia had been. That would cost the democracies their last friends in Central and Eastern Europe. Rumania, Yugoslavia and Hungary would be compelled immediately to make peace with the Nazis, knowing that if they did not join them as allies they would be annexed as vassal states. The Italians would gather in what the Germans left; the vast empire of the Axis would sweep right across Europe, from Spain on the Atlantic to Constantinople commanding the Black Sea and to Memel on the Baltic. And after this huge military power was consolidated, it would turn on France and Britain, now crowded into the northwest corner of the Continent, desperately trying to hang on to exposed colonial empires of which both Hitler and Mussolini had often demanded a share. It is possible that such fears were exaggerated. Yet in his book, his speeches and his actions Hitler had done everything to convince the democratic nations that they were only too well justified. Chamberlain and Daladier now found themselves being bitterly criticized by their own publics for their Munich policy. The French and British peoples were tired of crises, tired of surrender, tired of a state of affairs which seemed to promise only perpetual fear, perpetual unrest, perpetual uncertainty. They wanted to see somebody call a halt. If Chamberlain and Daladier had done nothing, they would probably have been thrown out of office.

But if they were to do something, they would have to do it. They had tried the policy of vague warnings and half commitments and it had merely landed them at Munich. The only hope of stopping Hitler was to make it absolutely clear that if he went too far, France and Britain would fight. They did not want to fight a war for Poland—indeed, cut off from them as Poland was, it would be even more impossible for them to defend that country than it had been for them to defend Czechoslovakia—and they did not care particularly about Danzig or the Corridor. But they did not want any more violent changes, dictated at the point of a gun. If they made it perfectly plain that they would fight in such a case, then perhaps Hitler would be willing to negotiate the Danzig and Corridor question peaceably; even such a solution as he had proposed would be much less dangerous to Poland's future if it were peaceably arranged; the matter might be worked out as he had asked, and there would be no need for a war. On March 31 Mr. Chamberlain told the House of Commons that "in the event of any action which clearly threatened Polish independence" and which the Polish government felt that it had to resist with war, the British would "at once lend the Polish government all support in their power."

The next day, April 1, Hitler spoke at Wilhelmshaven. He violently attacked the British and told them in effect to mind their own business. One week

later there was a sudden flurry in Albania, the little
Balkan kingdom which had long been under Italian
domination. Italian ships appeared off its coast; Italian troops were landed; there was some scattered
fighting; Albania's King Zog, his young Queen and
the tiny princeling to whom she had just given birth
were in flight across the rough mountain roads into
Greece, and Albania vanished from the map even
more suddenly than the countries which had gone
before. So Mussolini, like Hitler, seemed to be on
the march again. Great Britain replied at once by
giving to Greece and Rumania the same guarantee as
she had just given to Poland. Should they be driven
to go to war to defend their independence, Great
Britain would fight with them.

The answer came in another speech of Hitler's on
April 28. He attacked the British for trying to "encircle" Germany and suppress her; again he advised
them to mind their own business, and he tore up the
Anglo-German naval agreement of 1935.* He attacked the Poles for having "rejected" his solution of
the Danzig question, and tore up the Polish-German
nonaggression treaty of 1934. There was no mistaking what that meant. The Poles would have to do as
they had been told or face a war. And perhaps it was
at this moment that the great war in fact became
inevitable.

To Hitler, the British guarantees to Central
Europe (which were backed up by the French)

* See page 132.

seemed almost as menacing as Hitler's own violence seemed to France and Britain. He saw the democracies as trying to "encircle" him, and to encourage the small powers which stood in his path to resist his demands and so prevent him from having his way in a part of Europe which he had decided was Germany's special field. Germany needed their resources and markets for her own military power and economic prosperity. Why should Britain and France, who had the resources of the world open to them, meddle with Germany's interests here? Britain and France both had great colonial empires which they had seized by force in the past. What right had they now suddenly to turn "virtuous" and prevent Hitler from using force to get what he wanted? And there was more to it than that. Nazi Germany so far had got all its tremendous gains by taking them. To stop now, to be peaceable, to negotiate, to achieve any further aims only in accordance with agreements to which Britain and France did not object, would be a tremendous confession of weakness. It might well mean that Germany would get nothing more at all. The Nazi party, moreover, had seized and held its power within Germany by constantly pressing forward from one ruthless success to another. To stop, to be reasonable, to seem to yield to Britain and France, might well break up the party and be the end of Hitler.

Chamberlain and Daladier were willing enough for Hitler to have Danzig and the Corridor, but felt that they could not let him take them by force. Hitler might have been willing to stop with Danzig and the Corridor, but felt that he had to take them by force, without seeming to "ask permission." And the situation was even more dangerous than that. The surrender at Munich had convinced Hitler that Britain and France—since they had failed to fight for Czechoslovakia, where the military problem was simpler and the issues more important to them—would never fight for Poland if only Hitler himself were ruthless enough. But it had convinced Britain and France that—since surrender had proved useless—the one way to prevent a war was to make Hitler believe that they would fight. From that time on, the more tense the Polish situation became, the more Hitler felt it to be imperative that he force through his demands at all costs; and the more deeply did Britain and France commit themselves to war in case he did so, as the only hope of preserving the peace. Together these two tendencies made war all but certain; one more, and final, complication was to bring it about.

When Mr. Chamberlain announced the Polish guarantee on March 31, he probably thought it would be enough, that the Corridor question would be peaceably settled and that the guarantee would never have to be made good. At any rate, it seems to have been only after the guarantee had been given, and when Hitler's uncompromising and warlike reaction to it came, that the French and British realized how necessary it was that they should be able to make it good. But how could they do so? There was only one way in which any real military help could be brought to the Poles. And that was by bringing Soviet Russia into an agreement to fight on their behalf. In September, 1938, the democracies had rather rudely pushed Russia out of their affairs and out of Europe. In April, 1939, they were negotiating at Moscow to bring her back again.

Russia would be even more directly threatened by a German attack on Poland than she had been by the attack on Czechoslovakia. The Germans were as violent as ever about Communism; and even as late as his April 1 address Hitler was still talking about "this worst form of bolshevistic threat" and calling it the "Jewish Bolshevik pest." In spite of what had happened at the time of Munich, there seemed plenty of reason for Stalin to put his strength behind the "stop-Hitler front" which the democracies were trying to set up.

But the negotiations dragged; there seemed to be endless hitches. On May 3 the world was startled to learn that Litvinoff, the Soviet Foreign Minister, who had always been one of those most actively in favor of an alliance between Russia and the Western democracies, had been dismissed from office and his post taken over by the Premier, Molotoff. Some people remembered Stalin's curious speech on March 10 * and began to wonder. Some recalled the old idea

* See page 238.

that one day Germany and Russia would come together. It had been in the back of people's minds ever
since the Treaty of Rapallo, just after the World
War; * and even after the rise of the Nazis—whose
system, at bottom, was so much like that of Stalin's
Russia—it had never been forgotten. Some recalled
the rumors earlier in the year that something of this
sort was about to happen. But the notion still seemed
fantastic; if the Russians were making difficulties
with France and Britain, it was only because they
distrusted the democratic statesmen and wanted to
make quite sure that the latter were not merely trying to get Russia to do their fighting for them. The
British persevered. Perhaps at this time Stalin was still
in fact intending to join the "stop-Hitler front" and
was only trying to frighten the democracies into
raising their price and giving more definite pledges
on their own side. But what the British and French
did not know was that he had already opened secret
negotiations with the Germans.

The discussions at Moscow dragged on through
May and through June. Not all the difficulties came
from the Russian side. The British were not as eager
as they might have been. They sent only inferior
diplomatic officials to negotiate, not their Foreign
Minister. They retained a great deal of their old distrust of Communism, and the Poles—for good reason,
as it turned out—felt even more. Everyone would
have been happy if Russia had agreed to send its

* See pages 22 and 177.

great air force to the defense of Poland, which had practically none; but the Poles had no desire to invite in Russian infantry, which might never get out again. The weeks went by; people began to wonder even more whether there ever would be a Russian treaty, and to wonder how the democracies were going to save Poland if there were none.

The Germans, meanwhile, were giving all the signs of organizing against Poland another of their now familiar attacks. The German press and radio were chorusing their denunciations of the Poles in the familiar way; "atrocities," of the familiar kind, committed by Poles against German inhabitants of the country were being discovered and exaggerated; the "wrongs" of Danzig (to which the Germans had paid little attention from 1934, when the nonaggression treaty was signed with Poland, right down to the beginning of 1939) were being exploited. A not very important dispute between Poland and the Free City of Danzig (whose government had long been completely Nazified and wholly under Hitler's orders) about the local Polish customs guards, was being worked up into a crisis. Under cover of this crisis, a "defense corps" was being organized at Danzig; arms were being poured into the city from Germany along with what seemed to be large numbers of German SS men and soldiers. All this was on the ground that the city had to be prepared to defend itself if the Poles should suddenly try to seize it. But it was just as good preparation for a stroke by which

Danzig would declare itself a part of Germany and then defy the Poles to interfere.

In the last days of June it looked to the British as though the greater crisis was about to be precipitated in this way. They warned the Poles to be ready; and the Foreign Minister, Lord Halifax, made an impressive speech intended to convince Hitler that this time the British meant business. There were, he said, two fundamental purposes behind British policy. "One is determination to resist force. The other is our recognition of the world's desire to get on with the constructive work of building peace." Great Britain would be ready for the second as soon as it was convinced that the Germans were, too, and would then discuss all the economic and other problems which Hitler had raised. But "our immediate task is to resist aggression. I would emphasize that tonight with all the strength at my command so that nobody may misunderstand it."

There was no crisis. June gave way to July. Nothing irreparable happened at Danzig. The Moscow negotiations still went on; the British had got no treaty, but they had not definitely been refused one, and presently a Franco-British military mission started for Moscow, though in a very leisurely way, to agree upon just what military assistance Russia could bring to Poland if a treaty were signed. All Europe waited, in very lovely summer weather. Many people believed there would be no war—Hitler might not take Danzig after all or, more probably, if he did the French and British would never fight. Many others believed that a great war was now inevitable. But all, whether they thought it was inevitable or not, talked and thought of war and of very little else. There was no other politics, no other economics, no other social question in Europe but war. The arms factories roared louder than ever; more and more airplanes filled the skies; there was hardly a family without some man in uniform or waiting to be called up upon a word; there was not an apartment house without its air-raid warning signs, not a householder who did not have his or her place somewhere in the vast machinery of defense or of destruction that now stood ready for the signal. No one wanted war; but everyone was ready for it, and no one now hoped to stop it should it come.

Through July Europe waited. Perhaps there would not be a war. But it was easy to see that the Germans were very confident that they would have Danzig and the Corridor sooner or later and that the French and British would back down, while the French and British were very certain that whatever they did this time, they could not back down again. Anything was better than this situation; the democratic peoples had had enough. It was a deadlock which, if not broken, could only result in war. Perhaps because he sensed the fact, Hitler now prepared to break it by playing his last and greatest card.

On the 9th of August the German government intervened directly in the dispute between Poland

and Danzig; the Poles realized how bad a sign this was, and told the British that they believed a serious crisis would come before the month was out. Two days later the pro-Nazi High Commissioner of Danzig (officially he was an officer of the League of Nations) was summoned to Berchtesgaden for a long talk with Hitler. At the same time Count Ciano, Mussolini's son-in-law and Foreign Minister, arrived at Salzburg, where he was closeted with the German Foreign Minister, von Ribbentrop. What he heard probably surprised him. Everything that was said on both sides is not known. But one thing, among others Count Ciano heard, was that the Germans had now made up their minds that they could not "solve" the Polish question without a war—on Poland. The Italian apparently told his German colleague that to attack Poland would bring on the European war; it made no difference to von Ribbentrop. Italy made it clear that she would stay out of what was about to follow.

Five days later, on August 15, Sir Nevile Henderson, the British Ambassador at Berlin, was told by a high Foreign Office official that Polish "oppressions" and "persecutions" of the German minority were reaching the limit, that Poland was "running with her eyes shut to ruin," that it was only because of the British guarantee that the Poles were resisting Germany's demands, and that the Germans did not believe the British would fight for the Poles regardless of "whatever folly" they might commit. The

Ambassador replied that the Poles had been very moderate and that if they were forced to war in self-defense there was no doubt that Great Britain would fight. But the German "seemed very confident" and told the Englishman that not only would the Poles get no help from Russia, but Russia would probably in the end join in carving up Poland. Six days later, the great card was played. Late on Monday evening, August 21, it was suddenly announced from Moscow that Nazi Germany and Communist Russia had agreed to conclude a nonaggression treaty. Von Ribbentrop would arrive in Moscow on Wednesday, the 23d, to complete the negotiations.

It was a stupendous sensation. What the announcement really meant, no one knew; but what it might mean was clear to all. The bottom was knocked out of all the long British and French negotiations for Russian aid. If war came now, Russia would presumably be neutral; France and Britain alone could not hope to save Poland from the west; she would almost certainly be overrun sooner or later by the Germans, and could be saved, if at all, only by first beating Germany in a major war and then forcing her to give Poland back her independence. But was that all it meant? Was this the famous Russo-German alliance at last? Was Stalin planning simply to remain coldly neutral, or was he planning to join forces with the Nazis, to give them active economic aid if a war should come, perhaps even to fight with them as an ally? No one could tell until the proposed treaty was signed and published. But that this development was, at very best, a staggering blow to the "stop-Hitler front" was plain at once.

And the purpose of it seemed plain to the British and French statesmen. Hitler was planning to win the whole vast game at a single stroke—and without the major war that otherwise seemed inevitable. He would not stop now simply with Danzig and the Corridor. In a short, quick war he would crush Poland itself, at the same moment that he paralyzed the democracies by snatching away from them the hope of Russian aid and presenting them with this threat of a Russo-German alliance. The democracies would certainly never fight in face of this; and with the triumph over Poland, Hitler's mastery in Europe would be beyond challenge. This much was clear. The appalling difficulties of fighting without the Russians were clear as well; but it was also clear that perhaps the one chance of foiling the scheme was for the democracies boldly to commit themselves to war, with Russia or without Russia, come what might. Perhaps that would convince Hitler at last; and it was quite possible, anyway, that the announcement of the coming treaty was largely bluff. The British might have waited to find out from the terms of the treaty. But to hesitate even for a moment would give the appearance of weakness and so risk everything. On August 22, Mr. Chamberlain wrote a personal letter to Adolf Hitler: "Whatever may prove to be the nature of the German-Soviet agreement, it cannot alter Great Britain's obligation to Poland. . . . If the case should arise, [the British] are resolved, and prepared, to employ without delay all the forces at their command."

The Germans tried to delay the delivery of this letter until their Russian agreement should be completed; but the British Ambassador succeeded in bringing it to Hitler at Berchtesgaden on the afternoon of Wednesday, the 23rd. At the moment, people in Moscow were gaping at the strange sight of the Red Flag and the Nazi Swastika flying side by side. Von Ribbentrop was shut away in the Kremlin, at which he and his associates had flung so many insults, negotiating the treaty. In the mountain house at Berchtesgaden, the ambassador was finding the Führer "excitable and uncompromising"; he talked in "violent and exaggerated" language about Polish "persecutions" and "atrocities" against "his" Germans; delivered "tirades" against the British support to Poland and against the British press, and declared that he "did not desire war but would not shrink from it if necessary." The same evening von Ribbentrop and Molotoff signed their nonaggression treaty and the text was given out. It was more sweeping than most had expected. The Russians had made a complete reversal, had fully joined their policy with Germany's and had seemingly left no loopholes. But the democracies by that time were committed. Unfortunately, so, in his own mind, was Hitler.

One furious and anxious week was to follow. It

was a week filled with desperate negotiations, flying
diplomatic telegrams, interviews, letters—"That Hitler," M. Daladier is said to have exclaimed over one
of the Führer's outpourings, "he is a torrent!"—
plays for time, plays to put the blame on the other
side. It made little difference. Hitler's great stroke
had failed; the democracies had not been shaken by
Russia's sudden switch and held their ground. The
democracies' firmness had failed as well; Hitler had
not been intimidated into halting his attack on
Poland, and refused all proposals for negotiation
which would not have given him the power to dictate the outcome. Under the circumstances, there
could be but one end. With the German armies
steadily massing on the Polish frontiers, with France
and Great Britain calling up their reserves and insti-
tuting war measures, with the Nazi press and radio
filling the whole air with their stories of Polish
"atrocities" and "terrorism," with border "incidents"
piling up, the frantic but futile negotiations went on.
They included some strange scenes. There was the
interview between Hitler and the British Ambassador, when the Nazi Führer said that he was "by
nature an artist and not a politician, and that once
the Polish question was settled he would end his life
as an artist and not as a war-monger." But the ambassador "derived the impression that the corporal of
the last war was even more anxious to prove what he
could do as a conquering generalissimo in the next."
There was the moment when an apparent readiness

to negotiate on Hitler's part was suddenly changed by the appearance of new Polish atrocity stories, which the British Ambassador suspected had been "planted" in the Nazi press by Hitler's more radical advisers in order to hurry him on into war. There were many "diatribes" from both Hitler and his Foreign Minister. But there was never any real chance of peace.

The Russian treaty was signed on Wednesday, the 23rd. The British Ambassador found reason to believe that Hitler had ordered the invasion of Poland on the night of the 25th-26th. Instead, on that Friday afternoon the Führer despatched a communication to the British: "Poland's actual provocations have become intolerable. . . . If the Polish government denies responsibility that only goes to show that it no longer itself possesses any influence over its subordinate military authorities." Germany was "determined to abolish" these conditions along her Polish border in the interests of quiet, order and European peace; but on these and some other terms was willing to make a settlement with Britain. The British answered on Monday by urging Hitler to enter into direct negotiation with Poland. On Tuesday evening, Hitler, in a long and belligerent document, agreed to receive a Polish emissary, if he came with full powers and arrived next day. The time was exceedingly short; and the Poles, remembering how rapid were Hitler's methods and what had happened to Schuschnigg and Hacha after such invitations, hesitated.

That Wednesday evening the British Ambassador saw von Ribbentrop; the Nazi Foreign Minister produced another long document, containing the German demands on Poland, gabbled it off "at top speed" in German, and then refused to hand it over, as was customary, to the ambassador. It was too late, he said, as the Poles had not sent their emissary. The demands were not, in fact, unreasonable; but they never reached Poland and seem to have been prepared only to make a record that would look well afterward. Next day, Thursday, August 31, the Polish government sent its ambassador in Berlin to von Ribbentrop to say that Poland would enter into direct negotiations. The Foreign Minister did not receive him until the evening, and then found that the Pole had no powers to negotiate himself. The Germans announced that they had waited two days for a Polish emissary; since none had appeared, they took this as a rejection of their demands—which they now broadcast to the world. But already the orders had been given to the German Army and air force to advance. By dawn next morning the German bombs were crashing on Polish towns, and the German-Polish war had begun.

It was Friday, September 1. Once more Hitler had moved to enforce his demands by violence. France and Great Britain were irrevocably pledged, if he did so, to come to Poland's aid. Over and over again they had declared that if a forcible solution were imposed, they would fight without hesitation. The great mass of the people in both countries were convinced that their own national safety permitted no other course. Even if their leaders had wished to do so, they could not now turn back. One last "warning" was issued by London and Paris, to which the Germans paid no attention. On Sunday morning, September 3, the British ultimatum was handed in at Berlin. Unless Germany agreed within two hours to halt its attack on Poland and evacuate the country, Germany and Great Britain would be at war. Two hours later they were. The French, following a similar procedure, issued their declaration of a state of war the same afternoon, and the great war in Europe had begun.

It was just twenty-one years, lacking two months, since the great silence had fallen over the Western Front and the last European war had reached its end. The babies who were being born as the statesmen assembled in Paris to establish their new world, were just coming to their maturity as that world went up in the flames of still another general conflict; and they were now filling, in their thousands, the ranks of the new armies whose task it would be to make yet another peace.

A NOTE ON FURTHER READING

AMONG THE GREAT NUMBER OF BOOKS
and pamphlets on the last twenty years of European
history, a few are mentioned here which seem particularly useful or interesting. To all of them I would like
to acknowledge my indebtedness.

One of the best brief summaries is given by Vera
Micheles Dean in *Europe in Retreat* and *Why Europe
Went to War* (a World Affairs Pamphlet). Other
general accounts are *A Short History of the World
Since 1918* by J. Hampden Jackson; *Europe Since 1914*
and *Major European and Asiatic Developments Since
1935* by Walter C. Langsam; *Twenty Years' Armistice,
1918-1938* by William Orton.

Probably the best and clearest book on reparations
and war debts is *War Debts and World Prosperity* by
Harold G. Moulton and Leo Pasvolsky. For the rise of
Nazism, there are *Germany Puts the Clock Back* by
Edgar Ansel Mowrer and *The Nazi Dictatorship* by
Frederick L. Schuman.

A good, but unfriendly, account of Mussolini and
Fascism is *Sawdust Caesar* by George Seldes. An excel-
lent account of the Ethiopian War is found in *Italy
Against the World* by George Martelli. A good book

about both the Ethiopian and Spanish fighting is *Two Wars and More to Come* by Herbert Matthews.

Inside Europe by John Gunther gives many pictures of the personalities and events of the middle and latter part of the period. Much of the general story of Austria and Central Europe is in *Plot and Counter-Plot in Central Europe* by M. W. Fodor.

Frederick L. Schuman's *Europe on the Eve, The Crises of Diplomacy 1933-1939* is a very detailed but at the same time exciting account of the collapse of the post-war system, down to the Munich crisis. It is strongly hostile, however, not only to the Nazis and Fascists but to Chamberlain and Daladier.

Probably the best book on the destruction of Austria is *Betrayal in Central Europe* by G. E. R. Gedye; while the story of the Munich crisis is clearly told by Hamilton Fish Armstrong in *When There Is No Peace*. For the final crisis over Poland there is Mrs. Dean's pamphlet, *Why Europe Went to War*, which was mentioned above; while *The British War Blue Book* and *The French Yellow Book* are much more interesting reading than one might think.

W. M.

INDEX

No listings are given for France, Germany or Great Britain, as desired references to these countries can be more easily found under topic heads or under their leading statesmen. Other nations are indexed by name.